HOME
WORK

ANNA YUDINA

HOME / WORK

DESIGN SOLUTIONS FOR WORKING FROM HOME

With 450 Illustrations

Thames & Hudson

CONTENTS

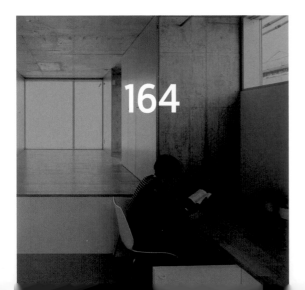

56

112

214

INTRODUCTION

In our hyper-connected world, the option to not only work from home, but also from literally anywhere, is becoming the reality for a growing number of people. The debate about the benefits and challenges of home versus office is ongoing, but it is likely that we will settle on a healthy balance between the available options: working in offices, co-working spaces, at home and on the move – in short, any place that is fit for purpose and suits the individual.

Work flexibility seems to be tied to boosting productivity and quality of life, and the ability to do so was recently found to be the number-one factor for millennials when making career choices. Recent research by Global Workplace Analytics reveals that 80–90 per cent of the US workforce 'would like to telework at least part time', and believe that two or three days per week would ensure the right proportion of concentrated work at home and collaborative work in the office.

In the Netherlands, a million homeworkers (out of a total population of 16.9 million) were recorded in 2015. Since 2016, Dutch legislation has allowed employees to request a change to their place of work, to include their homes.

In the US, FlexJobs has been active for almost a decade, and currently offers over 50 career categories to those seeking a job 'with some kind of flexibility', whether telecommuting, part-time, freelance or flextime. According to *Fast Company* magazine, 34 per cent of business leaders at the 2014 Global Leadership Summit London – which focused on 'Generation Tech' and its impact on global business – expected that more than half of their full-time workforce 'would be working remotely by 2020', while 25 per cent argued that 'three-quarters would not work in a traditional office by 2020'. The entire staff at web-development firm Automattic, best known for its blogging software and WordPress platform, work remotely across some 50 countries. Cloud services and various kinds of software are constantly being developed to further facilitate online communication and collaborative work.

The subject of flexible working is huge, and has a vast array of economic, social and psychological implications. This book focuses on the specific design challenges of working from home, and explores the striking variety of ways in which architects and designers are incorporating the workspace into the domestic environment, from transformable furniture solutions for small apartments to larger architectural interventions for managing the borders between work and other facets of life.

The projects included here are organized into chapters according to the tools and strategies used by the designers, with several strategies sometimes overlapping in one project. When seeing all of these designs brought together, what becomes most evident is the fact that each successful scheme reflects the unique pattern of the client's lifestyle and working habits, translated into a sequence of living spaces – with the workspace given just the right position, size, stability or flexibility, and degree of connection or isolation within this spatial story.

'It doesn't really have to be an office desk inside a home,' says Rianne Makkink of Dutch design practice Studio Makkink & Bey, longtime researchers into the various aspects of the workspace. 'It can be a kitchen table, on which you put some officeware, some extra items that add privacy or provide temporary storage space, and it feels more workable than a desk. And then, you change it again.'

Makkink confesses that for her and partner Jurgen Bey, the biggest insight was the importance of 'being present' to the place where you work; to your own behaviours and habits, as well as those of the people who work with you. As a designer, you see 'how you can react to it'. One example of the findings that result from such careful attention was cited in *Why* magazine, published by Herman Miller, a major manufacturer of office furniture: 'The notion of privacy ... has come up in thousands of conversations about office design, and yet the designers we spoke to pointed out that "privacy" has become a substitute word for "quiet" or "concentrated focus" – styles that don't actually require privacy, which is a much deeper philosophical notion. What we need may be an hour or two of quiet, or it may be silencing our phones.'

While revamping the offices for Starbucks, Andrea Vanecko, a designer at NBBJ, found out that using library-style tables was enough to clearly designate the silent zone. Applied to a home workspace, this might mean that the desired effect can be achieved with a series of meaningful details, from a boxed-in desk that creates a private bubble of concentration like the Bouroullec brothers' Diapositive or Torafu Architects' Koloro (pp. 230–1), to a blind that closes the desk off from the bedroom area during late-night work sessions in JAAK's scheme for a studio flat in Hong Kong (pp. 34–5).

This context-sensitive approach makes even more sense as designers seek to adapt to the large-scale changes that are affecting most of their clients. 'With laptops, tablets and smartphones becoming part of the household furniture, the former separation between work and living environments is diminishing,' notes Belgium-based firm Maf (pp. 202–3). 'Rising construction costs and new ecological insights have not only called into question monofunctional and occasionally used spaces, but also given rise to compact alternatives.' American architectural practice CHA:COL names dual use among their priorities for residential projects (pp. 28–9, 38–9). 'Lofts, especially historic lofts in Los Angeles, New York and San Francisco, are zoned for "artist live–work" use,' the team explain. 'This ordinance in downtown Los Angeles, for example, led to a huge boom in the adaptive reuse of older buildings, since it gave users the freedom to live and work in the same place. Interestingly enough, many lofts don't make use of such a powerful opportunity. In our loft projects, we like to demonstrate to users that (a) design solutions aren't necessarily expensive and (b) designing a space for dual use is an extremely functional and powerful tool.'

German designer Michael Hilgers sees his designs as 'solutions for dwelling challenges, such as narrow spaces – nowadays often caused by dramatically increasing costs for urban living space – and the change in the way we work today'. As oversized desks and bulky storage space become obsolete, Hilgers says, 'we are, or have to be, more mobile than ever before, and so does our furniture. Our homework devices are allowed to look like living-room furniture (p. 123), be almost invisible (p. 121) or even be a hybrid of a flower box and a desk to turn your balcony into an open-air office (p. 196).'

A possible next-level solution to shrinking apartments in coveted urban centres is CityHome, a project launched by MIT Media Lab a few years ago, which aims to 'develop, deploy, test and evaluate' technology-powered strategies for 'living large in a small space'. The prototype design was intended for an 18.6 m² [200 sq ft] flat; the list of experiences that would be improved via this single-unit, multipurpose, reconfigurable, remote-controlled robotic furniture system started with distributed work, and went on to include 'proactive health, energy conservation, entertainment and communication'. The first commercial product, branded as the Ori system, was co-designed with Yves Béhar's studio Fuseproject, with the first shipments slated for large-scale development companies in a selection of cities in the US and Canada.

According to workspace ergonomics research conducted by the furniture brand Knoll, 'knowledge work' represents the majority of work today, with almost half occurring outside the primary workplace. Even within our home, says Rianne Makkink, we are going to 'migrate much more'. Thanks to portable devices and wireless connections, we are no longer tied to a particular of the house. (If you tend to have your best ideas in the shower, why not use an integrated device to instantly record and upload them to the Cloud for sharing with your distributed team of remote-working collaborators?) Perhaps less obviously, being able to scatter the work process around different areas of the house has some ergonomic benefits, too. Knoll's research shows that casual lounge furniture allows people 'to naturally assume healthy work postures'.

Mason Currey, author of the bestselling book *Daily Rituals: How Great Minds Make Time, Find Inspiration, and Get to Work* (2013), has confessed in an interview with Prolifiko blog that, while writing his book in a draughty, poorly insulated apartment, he often dressed in several layers, and got used to wearing one particular hooded sweatshirt. 'Now I find I can't write without wearing this sweatshirt with the hood up,' he says. 'The hood acts almost like blinders – it forces me to concentrate only on the screen or page in front of me.'

With wearable technologies on the increase, perhaps one day a home-and-anywhere-else workspace will become as basic as that?

MOBILE

A home workspace can be seen as either an 'island' or a 'cloud': occupying a fixed, permanent position within the home, or capable of being moved or folded up to make room for other activities throughout the day.

A static, island-like design functions as a focal point around which various activities are organized. It can be the major space-maker in a home, and incorporate not just the home office, but other functions too. A live–work loft fitout by CHA:COL architects for a Los Angeles-based illustrator and creative director (pp. 38–9) consolidates in one sculptural volume a workstation for two, a sleeping deck and an intelligent clothing storage system. At the same time it liberates over 80 per cent of the 130 m^2 (1,400 sq ft) loft space for entertainment.

A similar approach is applied to much smaller homes, including a 32.5 m^2 (350 sq ft) studio flat in Hong Kong by JAAK Design (pp. 34–5). Here, the team has used the desk area – which forms the central part of a custom structure that also integrates the bed, wardrobe, plenty of storage and the bathroom/laundry block – as both the divider and connector for an open-plan living space.

In Montreal, an 'island' solution proposed by architect L. McComber (pp. 24–5) provided a professional artist with a much-needed but hard-to-locate studio space, and freed up an entire lower floor for her two children. Belgian firm C.T. Architects merged study and bedroom in the ground-floor loft apartment for a disabled client, who wished to lead an active and independent life (pp. 26–7). Meanwhile, a compact 'sleep + work' hybrid is an obvious solution for student rooms – as seen, for instance, in the designs of Graal Architecture (p. 20), Ben Allen (pp. 32–3) or Pieter Peulen (p. 219). Sometimes the desk and bed are just about the only static parts of a home, in which floor panels fold up to reveal hidden storage or pull out to become a table, as in DEFT architects' 25 m² (266 sq ft) scheme in Hong Kong (pp. 46–7).

As for clouds, they come and go – not unlike a workspace that emerges and retracts as necessary. Examples included here range from Konstantin Grcic's Hack system, with a sliding surface that transforms a standing desk into a sofa (p. 21), to Australian architect Nicholas Gurney's solution for a tiny apartment, where – in a conjurer-like move – the wall with a cantilevered desk slides through a cabinet to reveal the bedroom (pp. 42–3).

American architect Michael K. Chen sees 'dynamic scenario-based' interiors as a solution to living in densely packed urban centres. Projects like Chen's Five To One apartment in New York (pp. 52–3), or PKMN Architectures' scheme in Madrid, with archive-style cabinets that glide to create space for an office, a kitchen or a bedroom (pp. 54–5), use – to quote Chen – 'the exchange of volume between nighttime and daytime' to maximize the range of individual uses and experiences on a small footprint.

DESK PAD

ERIC DEGENHARDT
BOEWER.COM

This wall-mounted desk by German-based designer Eric Degenhardt creates a micro-office space with minimal means. Depending on the desk's placement, a side panel at the left or right minimizes distractions. The leather-covered writing pad, 1 m (3 ft 3 in.) long and 0.5 m (12 ft

8 in.) deep, is offset slightly to provide a convenient niche for storing books, files and other objects, with a storage compartment concealed beneath. Combining traditional and contemporary elements, Desk Pad integrates a book rest, pen holder and multiple socket strip.

LONGUE

MASSIMO MARIANI
TARGAITALIA.IT

This modular wall system by UK-based architect and designer Massimo Mariani has been developed around a homeworker's needs. To make efficient use of the wall space, Mariani designed three basic modules of unusually elongated proportions, each reinforced by a fixed aluminium 'bookend' and ready to be filled with functional accessories. Ranging in length from 1.6 to 3 m (5 ft 3 in. to 9 ft 8 in.), the modules can accommodate boxes of various sizes and colours, as well as a desk and drawers. The designer notes that each item comes fitted with felt glides so it can be easily rotated or shifted for the best arrangement and wiring of lamps, computers and printers. In addition to serving as a home office, the modules can be adapted to other uses throughout the home.

22 M²
APARTMENT

A LITTLE DESIGN
TAIPEI, TAIWAN

With its 22 m² (237 sq ft) area, this tiny flat may be smaller than many hotel rooms, yet designer Szu-Min Wang and her client – whose work requires frequent travel – were both convinced that, unlike a room intended for short stays, at home 'space is as important as function'. The renovation project was therefore focused on maximizing uncluttered space without compromising on the size and functionality of the furniture and equipment (including a full-size bath). The intensive use of the

3.3 m (10 ft 8 in.)-high wall allowed for a built-in wardrobe in its lower portion and bookshelves on top, accessible partly from the mezzanine, partly from a sliding ladder. The desk is located on the mezzanine, while on the ground floor a hinged table can either extend along the wall in a space-saving, bar-counter mode, or be folded outwards for dining or occasional reading and work. A pivoting lamp with a long 'stem' serves both the table and the adjacent storage bench.

ENCHORD TABLE

INDUSTRIAL FACILITY
HERMANMILLER.COM

Designed by Sam Hecht and Kim Colin of London-based office Industrial Facility, the Enchord table is 'rounded, rather than rectangular, and small enough to fit in a study but large enough for using laptops'. By adding a sliding secondary desktop beneath the main desk surface, the designers provided space for laptops, papers, peripherals, cabling and other work equipment while keeping the table's upper surface clutter free. The secondary desktop is also made 30 cm (12 in.) longer than the main one, and so can extend beyond the top surface at either end to form a side table or a shelf for a filing tray, printer or scanner. Combining a diecast aluminium frame with a top surface in white oak or laminate and a polyester-coated lower surface, the design 'mixes up the materials of the home and office'.

AA DESK

SPANT STUDIO
WOUD.DK

Danish architecture and design duo Troels Thorbjørnson and Kasper Baarup Holmboe developed the AA Desk to 'create optimal conditions' for today's flexible work style, enabled by portable digital devices. Their A-shaped design can be placed in the middle of a room, making it possible to work on either side of the desk, or to share it between two users. A shelf below the desktop stabilizes the structure and allows space for a quick clean-up to transform the workspace into a dining table. It also incorporates multiple sockets, while an LED light fixture rests on top of the desk's trestle-like structure to save desk space and illuminate the work surface.

APARTMENT IN PUTEAUX

GRAAL ARCHITECTURE
PUTEAUX, FRANCE

A multi-child family merged three flats into a 120 m² [1,290 sq ft] home in a suburb of Paris, and commissioned Graal Architecture to redesign the resulting space. 'Beyond simply reconfiguring the apartment's layout, we gave much thought to the different ways in which it will be used, notably the ways everyone in a large family could make this space their own,' Carlo Grispello, a partner at Graal, explains. The room, shared by four young children, includes a play area for spending time together, but each child's need for privacy and concentration has also been addressed. This was achieved with two custom-designed double-decker furniture units, each comprising two sleeping compartments complete with personalized shelves, some further shelving for shared use, and a workspace niche.

HACK FAMILY

KONSTANTIN GRCIC
VITRA.COM

This ingenious table system is aimed at young employees of high-tech companies, yet its customizable, user-friendly design would also appeal to a homeworker with a similar dynamic, no-frills attitude who values space-saving furniture. The project name, Hack, is a computer term that has come to mean a resourceful, 'often inelegant, but highly effective' solution to a specific problem that requires no fundamental changes to the wider system. In this spirit,

Konstantin Grcic has 'hacked' a traditional desk design to transform it into a three-in-one unit. Hack comes in a flat pack and consists of four fibreboard panels held together by metal parts to form a semi-enclosed workstation. Manually operated by means of a recessed grip or a crank, the tabletop height can be adjusted within seconds to serve as a stand-up desk, a 'normal' desk, or – in its lowest position and fitted with a few cushions – as a sofa.

INTERIOR
FOR STUDENTS

RUETEMPLE
MOSCOW, RUSSIA

Briefed to design a work and recreation room for two teenage siblings, Russian architects Ruetemple based their project on the idea of a dynamic recreation area versus a static workspace. A custom-designed ash-wood structure comprises shelving and personal desks for the sister and the brother. An integrated stair connects the workspace to the mezzanine, where the floor – except for the sleeping area – has been replaced with hammocks.

A piece of transformable cube-shaped furniture moves around the lower room on casters and can be divided into separate blocks to serve as a chill-out space, or two additional beds, and so on. A touch of dynamism is implicitly present in the design of the workspace, too: students can walk off the stairs directly onto a desktop, while a section of the shelves doubles up as a ladder, providing a shortcut to the hammocks above.

JULIETTE AUX COMBLES

L. McCOMBER
MONTREAL, CANADA

Initially required as a result of water infiltration, the renovation of the upper floors in a Victorian residence has led to a radically improved home for a young family. Juliette, a mother of two and a professional artist, needed a large, neutral, brightly lit studio, but none of the existing spaces in the house were right. Montreal-based architect L. McComber came up with a bold plan that replaced the old roof structure with an open-truss roof that raised the ceiling from 2.6 m [8 ft 6 in.] to 4 m [13 ft]. In addition to creating a larger space, enabling a band of southwest-facing windows and flooding the attic with indirect light, this solution has transferred the ceiling load in a way that completely liberates the floor plan. Today, the white-painted attic hosts the master bedroom and Juliette's studio. Making additional use of the 'utility volume', with shower and wardrobe housed inside, a wall-hugging piece of furniture reuses the century-old wood from the deconstructed roof and provides a workstation, complete with bookshelves and storage space.

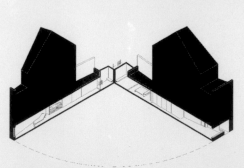

LOFT MM

C.T. ARCHITECTS
BILZEN, BELGIUM

Having only partially recovered after a car accident, this client of Belgian office C.T. Architects was determined to maintain an independent life – no easy task, as he was then in his late twenties and had a number of disabilities that turned the most mundane activity into a challenge. His new residence is a former garage and stockroom converted into a loft. The peculiar proportions – 3 m wide by 30 m deep (9 ft 8 in. by 98 ft 4 in.) – enabled a succession of increasingly private spaces, from a living/dining room to a bedroom/study, all packed with custom solutions. One of those is a hospital-style bed with a headboard that bends to form a cantilevered desk. Remote-control buttons for operating the bed and other electronic devices are integrated into a lamp, which swivels to light the desk or the bed.

WRITER'S BLOCK

CHA:COL
LOS ANGELES, CALIFORNIA

In their design for a live–work loft in the Arts District of downtown Los Angeles, architects Apurva Pande and Chinmaya Misra have created 'a compact urban oasis' in which the owners – an author and pianist wife and a game-designer husband – could enjoy periods of focused, occasionally collaborative work between frequent business trips. The resulting project was developed around a bespoke centrepiece, which acts as both a space divider and a multipurpose piece of furniture. Millworked from oak veneer, it was inspired by some of the clients' interests – namely, the space- and mind-bending architectural mazes of the game Monument Valley. As Misra noted in *Dwell* magazine, it can be used as 'a place to lounge, or as a place to retreat and write, or as a place to entertain, and sometimes as a place to just sit and meditate'.

DOEHLER

SABO PROJECT
BROOKLYN, NEW YORK

In the process of gutting and renovating this loft apartment, architect Alex Delaunay's team removed most of the partitions and the 1.2 m (4 ft)-deep drop-ceiling to restore the authenticity of the vast, airy space within an old diecast factory, which had been repurposed as housing in the 1980s. The new scheme boasts 3.6 m (11 ft 10 in.) ceilings. Fluid connections between all but the bedrooms, pantry and wet rooms 'expand each area beyond its limits'. This largely open space is dominated by a 2.3 m (7 ft 7 in.)-high storage wall formed of alternating boxes and niches, with an integrated study area and stairs leading to a newly added mezzanine.

A ROOM FOR TWO

STUDIO BEN ALLEN
LONDON, UK

Architect Ben Allen was tasked with creating an engaging space in which the client's two children could sleep, play and study during their stays in his flat. The design team responded with a single room that could be transformed into 'two interconnected but distinct spaces'. Inspired by Antonello da Messina's *St Jerome in his Study* [*c.* 1475], the project is a hybrid of furniture and architecture. Structurally, it was designed as a kit of CNC-cut plywood parts, easy to assemble and dismount. Reflecting the elder sister's greater independence and need for a quiet study space, her workplace is more private. Desks and step shelves can be moved or folded away to provide space to play.

KEVIN

JAAK DESIGN
HONG KONG, CHINA

For this 32.5 m² (350 sq ft) flat, the architects at JAAK removed the partitions that split it into five compartments to create an open-plan studio. Like their other projects, this design addresses the gap between Hong Kong's growing number of DINK (dual-income, no kids) couples and the lack of housing specifically for this demographic. Believing that 'partitioning is not the only way to create privacy', co-founders Calvin Cheng and Wing Chung Chau have alternative solutions that offer their clients 'both privacy and spatial experiences'. The flat is organized around a custom-built, prefabricated cabinetry block that incorporates a workspace, bed, wardrobe and TV block – all with plenty of storage and a passage along the windows to maximize natural light. An opening above the desk heightens the sense of connection, but can be curtained off when one partner needs to work late.

APARTMENT XIV

STUDIO RAZAVI ARCHITECTURE
PARIS, FRANCE

To redesign a classical mid-19th-century apartment in central Paris for a young couple – both passionate art collectors – architect Alireza Razavi chose to 'disrupt' the rigidity of the existing, structurally defined layout with an expressive, irregularly shaped, landscape-like piece of architectural furniture. Constructed from fibreboard panels, this black millwork feature snakes across the entire 80 m² (861 sq ft) flat, unifying the space and livening it up. The structure integrates a number of functions, including a workstation for two with a media wall, shelves and cabinets, and a bathroom complete with a sleeping loft at the top for guests.

36 STATIC / MOBILE

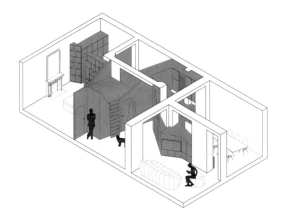

TOY LOFT

CHA:COL
LOS ANGELES, CALIFORNIA

For their newly purchased loft in downtown Los Angeles, a creative director and illustrator needed a live–work solution, in which areas for sleeping and storage would be consolidated to leave maximum free space for work and entertainment. A super-compact 'loft within a loft' that occupies, together with the bathroom, about 20 per cent of the entire space was the architects' response to the brief. The unit integrates a rolling, archive-type wardrobe, an extended work surface and a 'hybrid custom/Ikea' system of tiered box shelves that contain work items, serve as seating and connect to the overhead sleeping nook-cum-laptop bench. With both architects and clients 'educated in design studio environments, where you work, sleep, lounge, eat, produce and entertain in one interconnected area', the team say that in developing this project, 'each intuitively knew how the other would possibly use the desk, step or cubby areas for their work'.

LUOTO

SAMI RINTALA
DANESEMILANO.COM

With his mobile, multipurpose design, architect Sami Rintala set out to boost the efficiency of smaller apartments. Aimed at students and anyone else who needed to work and sleep in the same room, Luoto combines a desk, a bed and a few shelves within a footprint of 2.2 × 1.2 m [7 ft 3 in. × 3 ft 11 in.]. What's more, the work surface can also be used as a daybed for reading or simply chilling out, with additional storage space underneath, and shelves can double as a ladder. The designer explains that the 2 m [6 ft 7 in.]-high piece of micro-architecture is set on casters, so that it can be moved around the room, allowing the user to position it by the window during the day or withdraw to a quieter corner at night.

THE RENTAL

NICHOLAS GURNEY
SYDNEY, AUSTRALIA

Preferring to work with 'small, modest spaces', Australian architect Nicholas Gurney aims to provide dynamic solutions that are based on an intelligent organization of space. One of his recent projects is a flat in a suburb of Sydney, in which simple materials such as plywood and sheet steel were used to define and fit out work and rest areas on a tiny footprint of 23 m² (248 sq ft). It took just one carpenter to cut and assemble the kitchen, storage and bedroom blocks on site. A sliding partition with a cantilevered work surface closes off the bedroom nook during the day, creating a home office. Its operating mechanism is key to the entire project: Gurney used a wall-to-wall steel shelf that both conceals the sliding door track and supports the weight of the storage block in such a way that the desktop can seamlessly pass through.

DENGSHIKOU HUTONG

B.L.U.E. ARCHITECTURE STUDIO
BEIJING, CHINA

This renovated apartment in one of Beijing's traditional *hutong* neighbourhoods houses a family of six on an L-shaped strip of space, sandwiched between a two-storey building and a *hutong* wall. With a floor area of only 43 m² (463 sq ft) to work with, the architects from B.L.U.E. studio created a two-level structure, with a row of wooden boxes containing a living room, dining room, bedrooms and study spaces, occupying the ground floor. Each of these opens onto a shared, street-like corridor, lit via a full-length skylight, which creates an outdoor feel. The upper level contains a bedroom and play area. This spatial arrangement fosters a sense of familial connection, say the design team, while ensuring that each family member has sufficient personal space, despite the apartment's small size. To maximize the functionality of each room, the house is filled with fold-out and dual-function items, including a wardrobe that slides along rails to open up into a sleeping compartment at night or fold down into a seating nook, thus expanding the adjacent study space during the day (shown above and opposite, top and bottom right).

FLAT 8

DEFT
HONG KONG, CHINA

Arguing that a 25 m² (266 sq ft) flat doesn't have to be uncomfortable and cramped, architect Norman Ung of Hong Kong-based studio DEFT used exactly this footprint in a project that aims to achieve the same levels of comfort and functional capacity found in more spacious homes. 'Compact, functional in fitout, but methodical and easy to maintain' were his guidelines in designing Flat 8, in which all furnishing – except, perhaps, the prominently located and generously sized workspace – has multiple uses. Most of the living space rests on an elevated wooden platform, its height intentionally aligned with the bay window, which doubles as a reading niche. Storage compartments are concealed beneath the platform, while one of the wooden panels is in fact a hydraulically operated table that rises above it to provide dining space for two – or an additional work surface.

RED NEST

COUDAMY ARCHITECTURES
PARIS, FRANCE

Challenged to create an enclosed bedroom space, wardrobe and home office in an area of 23 m² (248 sq ft), architect Paul Coudamy solved the problem with the help of a mobile L-shaped shelving unit and a mirror. The wardrobe, bed, office shelves and fold-out desk, as well as four light fixtures, are integrated into a single, bright-red, high-gloss furniture element. During the day,

the mobile cabinet slides to open up the workspace and conceal the bed, masked by a two-way mirror at the other end. At night, the cabinet – with additional lighting from below – is moved to close off the office and switch the apartment back to 'bedroom mode'.

1 MOBILE SHELVING
2 BED
3 DESK
4 WARDROBE
5 BATHROOM

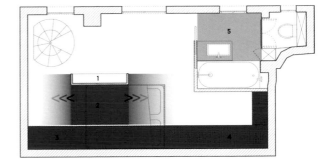

ISLINGTON MICRO FLAT

CIAO
LONDON, UK

The design for this 35 m² (377 sq ft) studio flat responds to the client's desire to be able to host friends and family – that is, up to four people – without compromising on comfort. Besides an open-plan layout that contributes to better natural lighting and makes the apartment appear more spacious than it actually is, the design team at London-based CIAO (Creative Ideas & Architecture Office) came up with a number of space-enhancing solutions. Among them is a bespoke, multipurpose furniture item that raises the floor in one part of the flat to contain a secondary, pull-out bed. When not in use, the bed disappears under the home-office unit, whose double-sided shelving with incorporated acoustic panels screens off another sleeping nook.

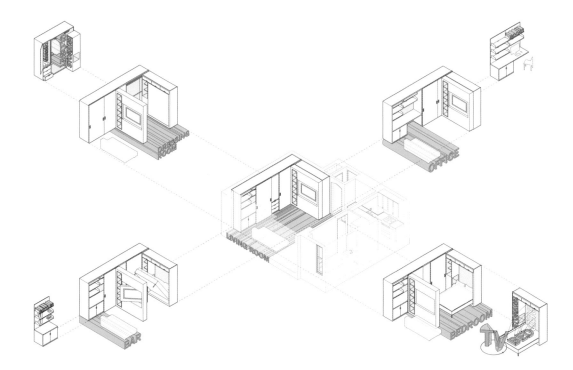

FIVE TO ONE APARTMENT

MICHAEL K. CHEN ARCHITECTURE
NEW YORK, NEW YORK

With their ongoing research into 'ultra-functional urban micro-housing', architect Michael K. Chen and his New York-based studio MKCA have developed expertise in 'transforming and moving architecture', which makes possible what Chen calls a 'transactional exchange of space' between day and night zones. This 36.2 m² (390 sq ft) apartment demonstrates his approach in action. A motorized partition slides between two walls to switch the room's functions between modes: bedroom,

home office, dressing room and living room. Additionally, this moving element houses a pivoting TV set, as well as all other audiovisual and networking equipment. By night, the sliding partition pulls to one side to make space for a fold-down bed; in the morning, it retracts to 'return' the space to daytime activities. The fully fitted home office is revealed behind the sliding doors of the built-in storage system; alternatively, the office can be closed off to enable dressing or lounge configurations.

ALL I OWN HOUSE

PKMN ARCHITECTURES
MADRID, SPAIN

When Yolanda moved to a one-storey house in a quiet residential community, she decided to divide this 50 m² (538 sq ft) space between her residence and her design studio. Today, the house that used to belong to Yolanda's grandparents is abuzz with friends, family, clients and foster cats and dogs. The new owner wanted to fit both home and work into a single space, while keeping these two aspects of her life 'relatively independent from each other'. Spanish architectural office PKMN – now split into two entities, ENORME Studio and EEESTUDIO – came up with a bespoke design that responded to Yolanda's brief, and also to her dynamic lifestyle. A series of storage units constructed from chipboard and suspended from the ceiling via an industrial railing system double as mobile partitions. Functioning in a similar way to mobile archive shelves, the system transforms the house throughout the day. The bathroom and the bedroom with its fold-out bed, the office space with a circular blackboard, and the kitchen open up when required and then 'implode' when not in use.

HORIZONTAL

VERTICAL

This chapter explores homework spaces as part of domestic landscapes. Some homes are designed as horizontal 'sequences' of various living areas, others as 'stacks' that result from the architects engaging with the entire available volume, including the vertical dimension.

In a 'sequence' home – of the type that translates its residents' lifestyles and domestic rituals into spatial flow, with different functional areas following one another in a specific order – the task is to find the most suitable place for a workspace within this scenario. For a New York-based photographer who wanted to use her residence as a living space, a photo studio, and a place to receive clients and showcase her work, but also to spend time with friends, architects Desai Chia developed a layout in which a gallery-cum-reception room – located just off the entrance – gives access to the diversified 'public' and 'private' zones (pp. 62–3), with the latter also including the photo studio.

Maxime Jansens's scheme for a loft apartment in Paris (pp. 66–7) ensures the mother's home office is strategically placed in the best-lit area, which is also a transitional zone between the children's rooms and the open-plan kitchen and living space. Japanese architect Keiji Ashizawa creates a sequence of home 'workshops' for a pattern-maker and a chef; the second is obviously a kitchen, and this provides a natural junction with the dining and entertainment areas (pp. 72–3). In London, Zminkowska De Boise architects used a snug comprising a library, a reading nook and a study desk as a connecting space between the two parts of a remodelled split-level residence – and discovered later that it had become the whole family's favourite place in the house [pp. 68–9].

In 'stacked' schemes, the workspace is often placed on the upper level, whether a regular mezzanine floor or a more radical arrangement like a desk suspended from the ceiling, as in Anna and Eugeni Bach's Gran Via project [pp. 76–7]. Similarly, ADN architects placed a home office and a bedroom on top of two freestanding volumes inside a loft apartment to allow for privacy when required, while also maximizing the transparency of the open-plan design [pp. 104–5]. Such a solution can also be the way to enable multiple uses within a limited space. Sometimes this comes with an extraordinary window view as a bonus, as in Isabella Maruti's scheme for an Italian lakeside villa [pp. 80–1]. Some designers raise the workspace as part of an eccentric, inspirational design [pp. 84–5], while others are asked to provide a homeworking parent with a vantage point from which to keep an eye on young children [pp. 86–7].

Finally, a vertical configuration can be the only efficient solution for a shaft-like unit with a high ceiling and a minuscule footprint [pp. 90–1, 92–3] – or a way to enhance a home by means of a double-height, atrium-like social space with interconnected eat–live–work areas [pp. 94–5, 96–7].

BERMONDSEY WAREHOUSE LOFT

FORMSTUDIO
LONDON, UK

Originally a 19th-century tin and zinc works, then an antiques warehouse converted into residential and business units, the building housed a two-bedroom flat owned by a photographer. FORMstudio was initially asked to make a few alterations to the existing design, but it was decided to radically revise it, as the owner wanted to emphasize the building's industrial character and scale. The result is a fully revealed, evenly day-lit loft space, measuring 17 × 6 m (55 ft 9 in. × 19 ft 8 in.), with all utility functions gathered within a single block in its corner, the bedroom concealed behind a sliding partition, and the kitchen island forming another compact block in the middle of the space. A full-width desk at the opposite end provides a work area with enough space to lay out photographic prints. There is a continuous cable tray along the back of the desk and a rail for hanging camera lenses above it.

PHOTOGRAPHER'S LOFT

DESAI CHIA ARCHITECTURE
NEW YORK, NEW YORK

A New York-based photographer briefed architects Katherine Chia and Arjun Desai to transform her cast iron-framed industrial loft into a 'serene environment', in which she could live, work, exhibit her photography and entertain friends. Her requests are met in this project, defined by an 'open-flow' layout with carefully thought-out lighting scheme and spatial sequences, and long axial views. Located just beside the entrance room, the library/

reception room [opposite, top] serves a dual function. It is a place for work-related meetings and creative research, as well as 'a hinge for two distinct zones in the loft', the architects explain. The east zone contains what they define as 'the private domain' – the photography studio and the master bedroom – whereas the south zone, meant as 'the public domain', comprises the kitchen, dining and living areas.

CLERKENWELL RESIDENCE

APA ARCHITECTS
LONDON, UK

Intended as an architectural portrait of its owners, opera and theatre director Dalia Ibelhauptaite and actor and director Dexter Fletcher, this 123 m² [1,324 sq ft] loft apartment is designed around a centrally positioned black metal cube. Inspired by the metal fire doors, left over from the 1930s industrial building in which the apartment is housed, the cube represents the empty black box of a stage. Designed to store films, books and the couple's archives, it also encloses the bathroom, which the flat's residents believe to be the most important place in the house, 'where one can seek absolute peace of mind and cannot be reached by the outside world'. The rest of the apartment wraps around the cube in a continuous movement, so that each of its sides faces a specific function: bedroom; workspace, with a custom-built, 4.2 m [13 ft 9 in.]-long desk in solid oak, kitchen/dining area and living room.

LOFT DP

MAXIME JANSENS ARCHITECTURE
PARIS, FRANCE

This loft apartment for a family with children, whose mother often works from home, occupies a former ground-floor workshop in a Parisian courtyard. In her renovation, architect Maxime Jansens used the loft's specific lighting conditions and the client brief to guide her when optimizing the 130 m² (1,400 sq ft) layout. The family asked for an open, generous space, as well as a home office for the mother. In practice, minimizing the partitions and fitting the few that were necessary with large panes of glass was an ideal solution for an apartment in which the natural light comes mostly from the glazed portion of the ceiling, and the children's room has no windows at all. The home office has replaced an old kitchen in the best-lit area under the glass ceiling. Directly adjoining the children's bedroom, it is also used as an extra playroom when the mother is not working. Respecting the tight budget and the family's desire to keep the space as uncluttered as possible, the kitchen, the long storage bench and the office desk have been merged into a single band of concrete and wood that stretches along the perimeter walls.

ROSE & JOHN'S HOME

ZMINKOWSKA DE BOISE ARCHITECTS
LONDON, UK

This 'HomeWork' solution resulted from a few alterations made by Zminkowska De Boise architects to the split-level ground floor of a home in one of London's conservation areas. The spine wall separated the living room at the front of the house from the lower-level dining room in its middle, making that room feel dark and disconnected. The clients' idea to cut an opening in the wall would have created an uncomfortable space with steps, hard to furnish and inhabit. Instead, the architects moved the dining area to the rear of the house and designed the steps with incorporated shelves that wrapped around the walls to form a bench seat by the existing fireplace on one side, and a desk on the other. Richard De Boise explains: 'We included a desk to enable the clients to more easily help with their children's homework and monitor them online. However, the new snug has become the centre of the home and family life, and the desk is used by all members of the family.'

HOUSE IN THE GARDEN

YAMAZAKI KENTARO DESIGN WORKSHOP
SAKURA, JAPAN

When architect Kentaro Yamazaki was designing this house, he sought to give its residents a sense of literally living in the garden. To achieve this, he took advantage of the location of the building, which is surrounded by greenery on all four sides. Arranged in a linear sequence, the various functional spaces – entrance hall, kitchen and dining room, bedroom, bathroom and study – are placed in five individual, differently sized blocks. Each block is slightly shifted off the axis so that spatial and visual continuity is maintained while also meeting a number of conceptual and practical aims. The gaps that result from this irregular arrangement are entirely glazed to maximize views of nature as one walks through the house. The absence of partitions blurs the mono-functional character of the rooms, while the shifting depth hides from view spaces that demand privacy or seclusion, such as the bedroom and the study, with the latter also being moved to the furthest end of the house.

FIVE BLOCKS:

1 ENTRANCE HALL AND WC
2 KITCHEN AND DINING ROOM
3 BEDROOM
4 BATHROOM
5 STUDY

AO STUDIO

KEIJI ASHIZAWA DESIGN
SAITAMA PREFECTURE, JAPAN

A young working couple – a clothing pattern-maker and a restaurant chef – wanted their flat renovated to make room for workspaces for both of them, and also for a lounge where they could entertain guests. By removing all existing partitions and concealing the bedroom, bathroom and various storage areas within a rectangular, sky-blue-painted pod, architect and designer Keiji Ashizawa's team could keep the larger portion of the apartment open-plan. Spaces for work and entertainment are arranged as a fluid sequence of specialized areas. The pattern-maker's studio is followed by the chef's testing ground – the kitchen, complete with a bar counter – and a lounge with a dining room, which opens onto a large outdoor terrace.

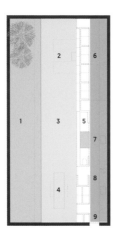

1 COURTYARD
2 BEDROOM
3 LIVING ROOM
4 DINING ROOM
5 SERVICE WALL
6 STUDY
7 BATHROOM
8 KITCHEN
9 ENTRANCE

MINIMALIST HOUSE

SHINICHI OGAWA & ASSOCIATES
ITOMAN, JAPAN

Shinichi Ogawa's design for this family home is defined by four 'strips' that stretch the entire 18 m (59 ft) length of the single-storey rectangular volume, which is topped by a slab roof. Incorporating the wardrobe, shower and toilet, the 9 m (29 ft 6 in.)-wide service wall divides the house lengthways into two major spaces. In each of them, different functional areas are arranged into fluid sequences, free of partitions. One sequence consists of the bedroom, living room and dining room and faces the courtyard, whose rear wall serves as a projection screen. The other is concealed behind the service wall. Here, a full-length cantilevered table in white Corian facilitates the second sequence: the kitchen, bathroom and – separated only by a protective glass pane – a home office for two.

GRAN VIA APARTMENT

ANNA & EUGENI BACH
BARCELONA, SPAIN

In this design for a 70 m² (753 sq ft) apartment in Barcelona, an elevated workspace with a hanging desk arose from the need to squeeze too many functions into a rather challenging layout. The owners of the apartment wanted to maintain two bedrooms facing the front façade, while the rest of the apartment – originally, three other spaces lit from the patio, plus two windowless corridors – had to accommodate a new living room, a kitchen, a dining room and a study.

Architects Anna and Eugeni Bach found a solution by removing the partitions to create an open, well-lit, multipurpose space, which forms the point of entry to the apartment. Taking advantage of the high ceilings, they located the kitchen inside a custom-made wooden box with a loft space on top, to be used as a study and occasional guest room. Occupying a corner space, it leaves enough room for a generously sized living and dining area.

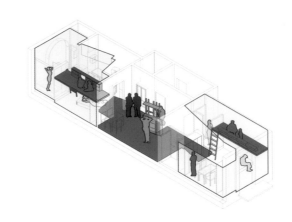

SALVA 46

MIEL ARQUITECTOS & STUDIO P10
BARCELONA, SPAIN

The long and narrow floorplan of this
65 m² (700 sq ft) apartment facilitated an
'experiment in shared micro living', carried
out by two Barcelona-based firms, Miel
Arquitectos and interior designers Studio
P10. The scheme defines two independent
units, each providing for basic functions
such as sleep, work and personal hygiene.
Placed at opposite ends of the apartment,
they open on to a space in the middle
that hosts social functions: cooking, dining
and entertainment. Sliding doors separate
private spaces from the shared central area,
allowing each resident to adjust the degree
of privacy depending on their mood. To
make the most of the 3.4 m (11 ft 2 in.)-high
ceiling, both workspaces have been
designed as mezzanines hanging above
the beds.

VILLA PINI

ISABELLA MARUTI
LIERNA, ITALY

Wherever possible, Isabella Maruti treats furniture as micro-architecture that 'defines the space and the ways to use it'. She has applied this design strategy to an apartment located on the top floor of a villa with a splendid view over Lake Como. The layout comprised a more conventional space, intended for the bedrooms and bathrooms, and a more open one, with the wooden structure of the gabled roof exposed, and a ceiling height of up to 5.3 m (17 ft 5 in.).

Here, the client needed to find room for the kitchen, the laundry and the study. To maintain the 180° panoramic view, Maruti proposed an open-plan design with a freestanding cubic volume that formed part of the kitchen, contained the laundry area inside and led, via the 'samba' stairs at the rear, to the workspace positioned on top. Nestled under the roof and providing a unique perspective, the study has become the most exciting place in the entire home.

M3 KG

MOUNT FUJI ARCHITECTS
TOKYO, JAPAN

This house for a manga film director and his wife, the president of an acting agency, resulted from a combination of the client's requests and the architect's ideas about a home as primarily a place of relaxation. The client wanted a large open space that would not look like a conventional living room; the couple also needed secure spaces for their film archives and art collection, while architect Masahiro Harada sought to emphasize the project's sensory aspects, rather than create 'intellectual'

white-cube architecture. In his design, the heavy, L-shaped concrete part conceals the private areas, while the living room – a soaring 6 m (19 ft 8 in.)-high and 5.5 m (18 ft)-wide space – uses a concrete wall as the backdrop to full-height, grid-like shelving made from engineered wood with a large grain pattern, and has glass walls on three other sides. The first-floor gallery, with sheet-steel floors, features a bridge suspended above the living room to serve as a study.

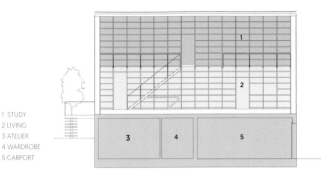

1 STUDY
2 LIVING
3 ATELIER
4 WARDROBE
5 CARPORT

ROOM
ON THE ROOF

i29 INTERIOR ARCHITECTS
AMSTERDAM, NETHERLANDS

Room on the Roof hosts the namesake artist-in-residence programme launched by the Netherlands' premium department store De Bijenkorf. Located in a small tower on the roof of the brand's flagship store in the historic centre of Amsterdam, the space offers its residents a telescope for enjoying panoramic views, and a unique experience of 'vertical living' in a 5.9 m [19 ft 4 in.]-high room orchestrated by interior architects i29. A floor-to-ceiling installation entirely covers one of the walls with a vertical arrangement of wooden box-like compartments that contain a study, a bed, a pantry and a storage box, all connected by ladders. With this design, i29 encourage the residents to explore the tower on different levels, each of them offering 'a new perspective of the outside world'. By contrast, the rest of the space, containing only a small lounge, is entirely white. A restored, full-height spiral staircase leads to the cupola and completes the project's Alice-in-Wonderland feel.

BOOKSHELF HOUSE

ANDREA MOSCA CREATIVE STUDIO
GREATER PARIS, FRANCE

This house in a Parisian suburb was refurbished to accommodate a couple with three children. The double-height living room was part of the existing design, but the place felt 'dark and indifferent' and required radical reinvention. The mother, an art-gallery manager, also asked architect Andrea Mosca to provide an enclosed office space on the mezzanine level from where she could keep an eye on the children. The family stayed with a friend while work on their own house began, and while there they fell in love with the bookshelf that occupied almost the entire length of their host's living room. This feature became one of the key elements that guided the concept. In the finished design the combination of a skylight, a glass wall and white surfaces fill the house with light. A bespoke bookshelf 'populates the space, playing different roles': it works as a room divider, a safety railing for the stairs, and as an enclosure and storage space for the mini-office.

STAIRS

FUGA_OFFICINA DELL'ARCHITETTURA
MILAN, ITALY

Architect Francesco Ursitti acted as his own client, builder and carpenter when he designed and executed the fitout for his family's ground-floor apartment in Milan. He took an ultra-minimalist approach that relied on basic forms and materials enhanced by an intelligent spatial composition. Except for the bathroom, the apartment is free of partitions, yet considerable ceiling height allows for a mezzanine floor that accommodates more intimate spaces such as the bedroom and home office, while the ground floor houses the double-height entrance hall/living room, with the kitchen further behind. Most of the furniture is made from fibreboard. Its shapes are defined by a cubic grid, often creating stepped configurations – whether a kit of actual cubes used as stools or assembled into other furnishing elements, or a bed with integrated storage and tiered seating. The mezzanine has fibreboard flooring, and the extra-long desk in the home office is made from the same material.

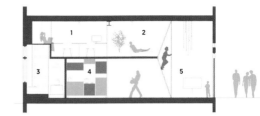

100 M³

MYCC
MADRID, SPAIN

The bizarre dimensions of this space – 100 m³ (3,531 cubic ft) for a footprint of 20 m² (215 sq ft) – are the result of its exceptionally high ceiling, which is also the only source of natural light. Challenged to transform it into a live–work unit for a young single person, Madrid-based MYCC architects have managed to provide a full spectrum of domestic functions while retaining a sense of space and luminosity; they also sought to make living here a unique and enjoyable experience. Inspired by platform-style computer games, the design uses a series of landings placed at different heights and connected by a variety of stairs. There are no partitions, and the landings are arranged to enable the entire apartment to be seen from almost anywhere. Each landing is assigned a specific function, although this can be flexible; the study – accessed via a wall ladder – doubles as a chill-out space and occupies the best-lit, terrace-like platform, with an operable skylight.

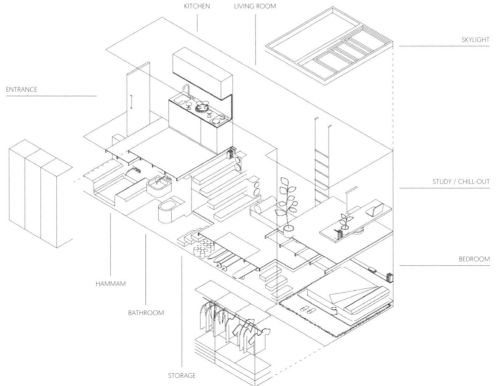

KITCHEN

LIVING ROOM

SKYLIGHT

ENTRANCE

STUDY / CHILL-OUT

BEDROOM

HAMMAM

BATHROOM

STORAGE

TOWER APARTMENT

AGENCE SML
PARIS, FRANCE

Fitting a four-room flat – including a home office – into a shaft-like space with a footprint of 25 m² [269 sq ft] and lit exclusively through the roof was the client's request for Marc Sirvin and Clémence Eliard of Paris-based firm SML. The two architects responded by treating the apartment as a tower in which each floor is dedicated to a specific function, from the bathroom in the basement and the kitchen/living room on the ground level, to the study and dressing room on the first floor, and the bedroom on a half-floor under the sloped roof. The floors are connected by alternating-tread stairs, a convenient and safer alternative to traditional steep stairs in tight spaces. The white colour chosen for most of the surfaces – except the warm touches of wood – maximizes luminosity, while the central void – together with the large openings in the stairs' design and the metal grid floor in the home office – allows daylight to penetrate through the entire volume, even reaching the ground-floor living room.

25 M², FOUR FLOORS
BASEMENT: BATHROOM
GROUND FLOOR: KITCHEN/LIVING ROOM
FIRST FLOOR: OFFICE/DRESSING ROOM
SECOND FLOOR: BEDROOM

ESSEX MEWS

MW ARCHITECTS
LONDON, UK

Tasked with designing an up-to-date alternative to a classic Victorian terraced house, architect Matthew Wood collaborated with independent developer Solidspace on a difficult site in a South London suburb. The trademark typology present in every Solidspace project is the split-level 'Eat Live Work' cluster, in which kitchen/dining room, living room and study are arranged over three half-floors and connected by short flights of stairs to create a unified, light-filled, double-height social space. Responding to the combined challenge of building on a piece of redundant, steeply sloping land in a conservation area, the team has delivered three homes whose height varies from a two-storey front to a three-storey rear. The humble exterior respects the 'surrounding vernacular' and contrasts with the 'large, bright and contemporary inside'.

MACKESON ROAD

MW ARCHITECTS
LONDON, UK

The owners of this property used to regard the half-storey height difference between its front and rear sections as 'an insurmountable problem', notes architect Matthew Wood, but his prior experience with the Essex Mews houses [pp. 94–5] helped him to turn it into an advantage. The same basic principle of locating a home's three key functions – eating, living and working – on three different levels arranged around a two-storey high void has been applied to the existing but fully refurbished house. This creates a shared, bigger and brighter space, in which individual rooms are better connected both visually and spatially. Another distinctive feature of this home is the wall storage by Uncommon Projects – designer-makers of bespoke plywood furniture – that spans two floors to serve both the kitchen and the study.

LINDA & JOHN'S LOFT

ZMINKOWSKA DE BOISE ARCHITECTS
LONDON, UK

A writer and his wife briefed Hanna Zminkowska and Richard De Boise to convert the loft in their Edwardian terraced house into a small study and library. 'The scheme is a modern take on the timber-lined rooms of houses from the period, with floors, partitions, ceilings, stairs, balustrades, handrail, and built-in desk and shelves all constructed with oiled birch laminated plywood,' the architects explain. Their project makes the most of the existing split-level configuration and amplifies natural lighting on both half-floors. On the lower level, the desk fits snugly into the niche formed by the newly added east-facing dormer window with a view over the suburban roofscape, while the upper level has been upgraded with two west-facing roof lights, seating and bookshelves.

EAST VILLAGE STUDIO

JORDAN PARNASS DIGITAL ARCHITECTURE
NEW YORK, NEW YORK

Brooklyn-based architect Jordan Parnass describes the essence of this project as 'carving a bachelor's studio into a live–work sculpture for a grown-up'. According to Parnass, in its original state the jam-packed studio flat – slightly under 46 m² [495 sq ft] in size – felt like a college dorm rather than a home. With the aim of remodelling the residence to efficiently serve the client's professional and personal needs, the scheme consolidated the kitchen, the bathroom and the sleeping loft into a compact, wood-panelled 'service core'. Both the service core and the adjoining wall are used extensively for neatly concealed storage. This leaves the larger part of the radically decluttered space free to be shared between the home office and the lounge, with the white, high-gloss surface of the full-height storage wall maximizing the luminosity and airiness of the new design.

HOUSE OF ROLF

STUDIO ROLF.FR & NIEK WAGEMANS
UTRECHT, NETHERLANDS

Dutch architect Rolf Bruggink collaborated with Niek Wagemans, a specialist in the creative upcycling of waste materials, to transform a 120-year-old coach house into a home and workspace for Bruggink and his girlfriend Yffi van den Berg (who also took part in the design process). Measuring 15 × 7 m (49 ft 3 in. × 23 ft) and 5.5 m (18 ft) tall, the structure was left unchanged, except for a panoramic window cut into its rear wall. Most of the living functions are contained in a freestanding, centrally positioned sculptural volume that houses a kitchen topped by a bedroom, a walk-in wardrobe, a toilet and shower room, plus a quirky cantilevered desk/bath arrangement. In developing the fitout, Bruggink and Wagemans challenged themselves to use up all of the materials from a dismantled shed that was part of the same property. Thus, two walls of the 'house-inside-a-house' are built from salvaged radiators, while the solid wood parts use reclaimed trusses, purlins and floor beams.

LOFT FOR

ADN ARCHITECTURES
BRUSSELS, BELGIUM

For this 96 m² (1,033 sq ft) loft, Belgian architectural firm ADN developed a masterplan of sorts. In an open space with white walls and floors and an exposed concrete ceiling, two freestanding and equally white volumes house more private domestic functions. With their walls made of metal sheets, the completely opaque ground-level parts of the volumes accommodate the bathroom and the laundry. The translucent and airy upper parts, protected by perforated screens, house the bedroom and the home office. There was no need to partition the rest of the space, as the volumes helped to define several distinct areas, including the kitchen block, stretching along one wall; a dining area, set up on a town square-like space between the volumes; a storage wall, placed close to the entrance; and a lounge/library tucked behind the bedroom volume and in front of a large window.

LOFT ON BUFALINI STREET

FABBRICANOVE
FLORENCE, ITALY

In the heart of Florence, under the barrel-vaulted, frescoed ceiling of a former music hall, Fabbricanove architects have designed a residence for a family of three. Revisiting Le Corbusier's concept of the house as a machine for living in, the scheme is defined by the 8 m (26 ft 3 in.)-tall 'core' that serves as a double-height, double-sided storage system, and much more. Its plywood walls form a bespoke, Mondrian-esque matrix of compartments and drawers. From a practical standpoint, it enables a variety of domestic functions, including a home office, without dividing the space into traditional rooms. Aesthetically, it is a strong contemporary element set inside a respectfully preserved historic setting. On the ground level, 'the core' encloses the pantry and the library/wine bar, while its exterior 'façade' lends itself to the kitchen and dining room. The glass-floored upper level contains the study and the playroom, but also provides storage for the adjacent master bedroom.

HOUSE LIKE VILLAGE

MARC KOEHLER ARCHITECTS
AMSTERDAM, NETHERLANDS

The outcome of lively discussions with the client, a couple expecting a baby, this 160 m² (1,722 sq ft) loft – once a harbour canteen on one of Amsterdam's islands – was designed as a group of small houses within a large one, with the possibility of adding further 'houses' as the family's needs evolve. Their arrangement and design – including the thick walls for smart storage – reflect the wife and husband's daily rituals. On the ground level, 'streets' and 'squares' formed by the mini-houses provide flexible space for spontaneous activities and socializing, but also let daylight deep into the space. Inside, the houses contain 'static', private functions such as bedrooms and bathrooms. 'Roof terraces' on top of these take advantage of the high ceilings and lend themselves to cooking, dining and office work.

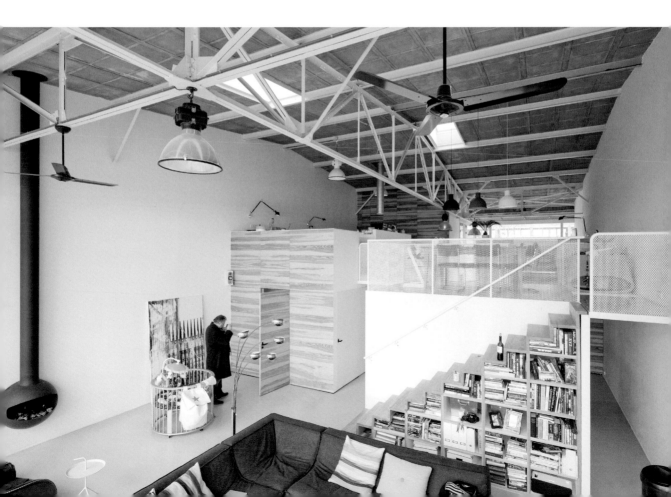

HOME/STUDIO KILBURN LANE

STUDIO McLEOD
LONDON, UK

A long-held dream of architect Duncan McLeod and his wife – to transform the ground floor of their London-based property and create 'an unexpected home and office behind an unassuming entrance' – has materialized into a witty, budget-savvy design that exemplifies the studio's creative thinking to inspire both the team and the clients. In the south-facing space, clerestory windows guide direct sunlight onto curved walls, rather than people's heads and computer screens. They also form balustrades for the garden on the studio's roof – a welcome addition to the existing house, which now has outdoor spaces on each floor. Glimpsed and reflected views, as well as 'hidden doors that allow varying degrees of visual and acoustic separation', make sure that home and work 'overlap without interfering'. Well-tempered daylighting and natural materials like the brick floor, raw plaster and oak-panelled walls, create a work environment that does not resemble a standard office and can effortlessly blend with the rest of the home should the studio move out.

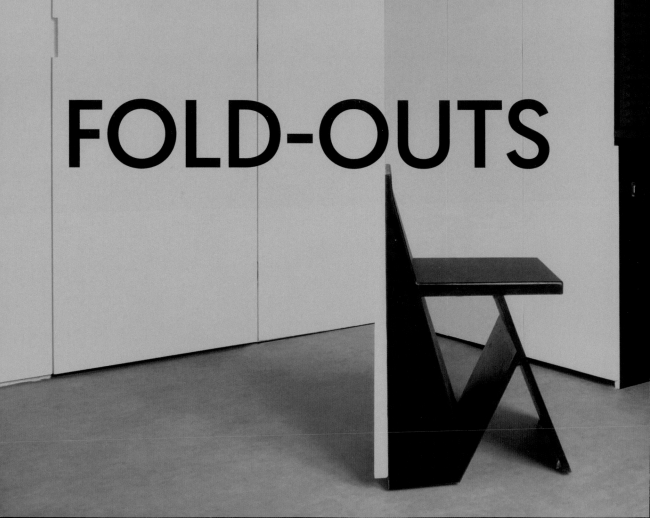

FOLD-OUTS

PARTITIONS

Compact, lightweight and wireless: our digital devices have done much to reduce the size of our desks and emancipate work routines. But anyone who spends any significant time working at home still needs to carve out a convenient workspace. There is also the need to balance work and home life, often with the additional challenge of having to accomplish it all in a small- or modest-sized living unit in a densely populated urban centre.

This chapter and the next explore the different ways in which design can help. Some of these schemes deploy smart room dividers and fold-out elements that have been instrumental in making the most of the space. In 2015, as a jury member of RIBA's House of the Year awards, architect Mary Duggan shared her observations on the trend for 'broken-plan living'. The evolution of the open-plan home into a more fragmented version of itself has been spurred by the use of personal digital devices and the resulting 'greater independence between family members', as Duggan told *Dezeen*. She went on to confirm that 'the increasing number of people choosing to work from home is playing a big part in the way houses are designed'.

Having discarded rigid partitions in favour of better-lit, connected living areas, the next step is to reconcile this with the demand for more articulated, intimate spaces. This chapter highlights designs that use various kinds of partitions to provide both this articulation and sense of intimacy in the workspace. Translucent, visually permeable or completely transparent (pp. 128–31, 136–7, 140–1); sliding, pivoting or folding up like a garage door (pp. 138–9, 140–1, 142–3); made from softly draping fabric or from the scaled-up headboard of a bed (pp. 124–5, 116, 126–7), they achieve these aims without sacrificing the general sense of openness or disconnecting the work area from the rest of the house. In the words of Spain-based ELII architects (pp. 142–3, 150–1), they are 'the divisions that allow continuity'.

In mini- and micro-flats, multifunctional, Swiss army knife-style furnishings – from individual dual-use items such as Michael Hilgers's Duotable (p. 122) to Spacon & X's fully fitted home office that disappears into a slot in the wall (pp. 154–5), or entire floor-to-ceiling systems like those designed by Michael K. Chen (pp. 156–9) – make it possible to configure the same patch of space for different uses. A space can change from bedroom to home office to dining room in a single day. This fits with the seven strategies for small but high-standard living formulated by Hong Kong architect Gary Chang, including engaging all idle surfaces to their full height and length, optimizing storage, and using multipurpose furniture and mobile elements for time-based transformation (as opposed to fixed zoning).

A wealth of time- and space-conscious, fold-down and slot-in solutions for homeworkers are featured in the pages that follow.

AREA

ALAIN GILLES
MAGNITUDE.BE

With his Area bed, Belgian designer Alain Gilles explores the different possible uses of a bedroom. There exist hybrids of a bedroom and a bathroom, a bedroom and a study, a bedroom and a lounge – so why not design a bed that contributes to a better way of organizing such dual-function spaces? The bed suggests a freestanding placement: its wide and tall headboard acts as a room divider, and can even bend backwards to form two lateral screens and thus define a secondary space open to a variety of uses. A series of add-on accessories includes a leaning 'pocket table' and a sliding double-sided lamp, which make it easy to use this 'room within a room' as a compact home office.

DESKBOX

RAW EDGES
ARCO.NL

When folded up, this cantilevered, wall-mounted item acts as a shelf and storage box. A parallel mechanism, similar to those used in toolboxes and containers for needlework equipment, expands it into a desk suitably sized for working on a laptop. Initially, Yael Mer and Shay Alkalay of London-based Raw Edges, in collaboration with Okay Studio, had developed it as a bread box, but the manufacturer soon recognized the project's space-saving potential, and so it has been rethought and repurposed as a micro-workspace solution.

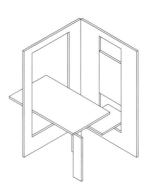

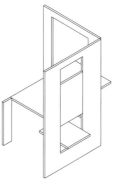

FLKS

KAPTEINBOLT
KAPTEINBOLT.NL

Interior architect Louwrien Kaptein and multimedia designer Menno Bolt – the two partners behind Dutch design studio Kapteinbolt – have designed a flexible workstation that packs completely flat when not in use. The item consists of plywood panels that all fold at 90° to form a kind of room within a room – with a desk, a chair and a screen marking out a place of concentration and ensuring some degree of privacy.

WALL

GILLES BELLEY

With his series of conceptual furniture pieces called Room (see also p. 232), French designer Gilles Belley explores such basic functions as sleeping, reading and working 'that will always be part of the mix, regardless of the sociological discourse on the shape of things to come'. Wall therefore clusters these functions around a self-supporting partition screen composed of vertical timber modules that become more stable once they are assembled. The screen can be configured to form any number of 'sub-spaces'; the modules have slots for carrying the consoles that support shelves or larger work surfaces.

FLATBOX

MICHAEL HILGERS
MUELLERMOEBEL.DE

Berlin-based architect Michael Hilgers draws his design challenges from the collision of two trends. 'Urban living gets more expensive every day, so city dwellers are forced to move to smaller flats. The other trend is that more people work from home due to massive changes in technology and workspace environments,'

Hilgers comments, on the reasons behind his interest in 'densifying functionality in a small space'. Flatbox compacts the workspace to a wall-mounted box sized 71.7 × 43.1 × 12.2 cm (28 × 17 × 5 in.) when closed. Mounted at any height, it can serve equally well as a standing desk or a child's workspace.

FLATMATE

MICHAEL HILGERS
MUELLERMOEBEL.DE

Flatbox's bigger brother, Flatmate, is another fold-out workstation by Michael Hilgers. The design makes practical use of 'leftover' spaces unsuitable for conventional furniture. With a footprint of less than 900 cm² (1 sq ft) and a discreet exterior that blends with its surroundings when the desk is pulled up, Flatmate can 'transform long hallways into home offices' or provide a temporary workspace in a weekend home. Despite its compact size, it can fit a fully equipped networked office with storage space for portable devices, integrated chargers and glare-free lighting, as well as two side flaps that reveal additional storage compartments.

DUOTABLE

MICHAEL HILGERS
URBANFAVOURITES.DE

Another space-savvy design for compact urban pads, this dining table seats four and converts into a home office in a single move. Duotable has 'a split top that opens on one side to reveal three differently proportioned compartments, including two A4-sized ones, and has storage space under the other side, while its steel base is shaped to allow for cable management', says designer Michael Hilgers. Much

thought was put into making every detail both functional and convenient. The cables are neatly hidden inside the hollow leg; the storage space under the front half of the table is designed as a pocket in which to store a laptop, a telephone or a book, decluttering the work surface while keeping them close at hand; and the flap-out half of the tabletop serves as a memo board or a rack for a tablet PC.

SETUP

MICHAEL HILGERS
MUELLERMOEBEL.DE

A further design from Michael Hilgers: the Setup cabinet was designed as a 'modular furniture kit' based on two basic modules – a rectangular and a square storage box, with or without a shelf inside – that can be assembled into countless space-saving combinations. The cabinet can be placed against a wall or form a freestanding, double-sided configuration. The larger module can be fitted with a fold-out desk with integrated lighting. In the back-to-back configuration, it can serve as a room divider and a workspace, providing individual desks for two.

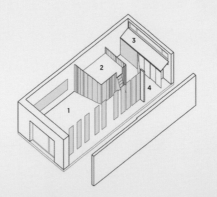

1 OFFICE
2 BEDROOM
3 KITCHEN
4 BATHROOM

HOME-STUDIO MQ 60

MKS ARCHITETTI
PESCARA, ITALY

Architects Fabio Mancini and Silvia Kliti needed an original and practical solution to transform a 60 m² (646 sq ft) warehouse into a home office for themselves and their practice. Wishing to create an airy, light-filled space, the design team opted for white curtains instead of rigid partition walls. The curtains softly drape and form fluid curves as they envelop the 'home' areas: bedroom, wardrobe, kitchen and bathroom. In the office part, they take the form of separate, vertically stretched

rectangles that slide to cover the storage shelves. 'The space, on the whole, is conceived as a piece of an Italian village,' the architects comment. The curvy passage evokes a small village street, while 'the smooth movement of the curtains gives the feeling of an infinite space.' The overall effect is of a maze, which in this project allows the design team to create 'a space without doors but with clear divisions' between private and public areas.

PLAZA KENNEDY APARTMENT

ANNA & EUGENI BACH
BARCELONA, SPAIN

In adapting this apartment to the lifestyle of its new residents, one of the key elements of the project was a space that had to combine the master bedroom and the home office. The smooth functioning of this two-in-one arrangement is made possible through a hybrid design that transforms the bed's headboard into a room divider, with office shelving incorporated into the other side. Tall and wide enough to screen off the workspace, it does not touch the ceiling and therefore allows natural light into the bedroom. The scheme's other crucial component is an enclosure made from wooden planks. Wrapping around the bedroom wall and ceiling, it gives an intimate feel, but also incorporates the ventilation system and ensures its silent operation, which is vital to the success of both the bedroom and the office.

WORKROOM

RUETEMPLE
MOSCOW, RUSSIA

Moscow-based architects Ruetemple have transformed a 35 m² (377 sq ft) garage space for a client who needed a comfortable studio for his daughter's artistic practice. Aiming to create a spacious, light-filled and inspiration-friendly workroom, Ruetemple's Alexander Kudimov and Daria Butakhina opened up the ceiling to expose the beautifully crafted timber beams, and custom designed an all-in-one piece of furniture that incorporates a large desk, a shelving system, a corner sofa and even an overhead sleeping berth. Shelving compartments of various sizes allow for storage of different paper formats, as well as gypsum heads and tools. Another workstation – a counter stretched along the studio's windows – offers meditative views of the garden as a welcome change of scene during the creative process.

BEN GURION BOULEVARD APARTMENT

DORI-DESIGN
TEL AVIV, ISRAEL

Originally, this 110 m² (1,184 sq ft) residence overlooking one of Tel Aviv's major avenues, within walking distance of the sea, was defined by small niche-like spaces, a long, dark and narrow corridor and a tiny kitchen located at the apartment's rear, far from the living room. The client brief called for a balcony lounge and a spacious public area with a home office connected to it – in other words, the existing set up had to be radically rethought. A three-month-long renovation process led by interior designer Dori Redlich resulted in removing 'almost every possible interior wall and eliminating all of the cubicles and hallways'. The new scheme is centred on an open, brightly lit space that unifies a large terrace, kitchen, and living and dining room fitted with 'various seating and hosting options'. The home office faces the public area, from which it is separated by a glazed screen. A curtain can be drawn across the screen to separate 'work' from 'home'.

SS PENTHOUSE

DE MEESTER VLIEGEN
ANTWERP, BELGIUM

De Meester Vliegen architects have converted a conventional penthouse into a private office with the possibility of later selling it, with no further alterations, as a residence for a couple with one child. The client needed a high-end, ultra-minimalist workspace away from his main office, in which he could work during the early morning and late at night and have private business meetings during the day. However, those were the only constraints. Completely stripped of its original divisions, the space is structured with the help of two custom-designed features. One is a centrally positioned block clad in glossy nutwood veneer and containing storage, the kitchen, the bathroom and the fire escape stairs. The other is a floating cabinet in green marble, complete with a cast-iron fireplace. The latter articulates the sitting room with its large desk, while the wooden block both serves and screens off a second office space together with a bedroom and dressing room.

LES ENFANTS ROUGES

UBALT ARCHITECTES
PARIS, FRANCE

Tasked with fitting out a flat in a 17th-century building, Nastasia Potel and Mylène Vasse of Ubalt Architectes had to arrange a domestic interior and a home office in 36 m² (388 sq ft), while creating the illusion of a larger space. The design scheme squeezes the kitchen and bathroom into a single service block in a corner, while the bedroom, protected by an accordion-pleated screen, is along the opposite wall. The central space hosts work and living/dining areas. Bespoke office furniture and a dining counter plug into the partition walls, and the historic wooden beams are exposed. The sequence of rooms and the mirrored vertical surfaces of the furniture, along with the linear light fixtures, visually expand the space in two directions.

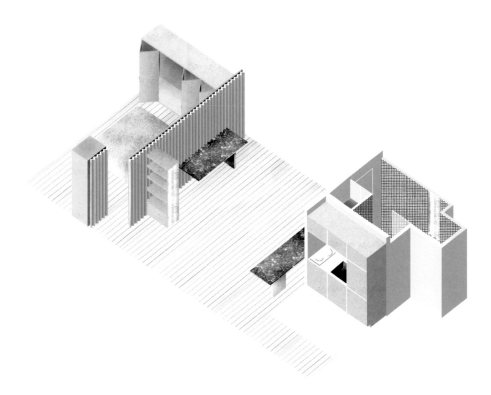

SCREEN HOUSE

STUDIO BEN ALLEN
LONDON, UK

The renovation project for this 65 m²
(700 sq ft) property in a 19th-century villa
in North London draws upon the owner's
wish to maintain individual rooms while
making them feel more flexible and
interconnected. Studio Ben Allen used
patterned openwork screens – commonly
found in traditional Indian architecture – to
form a cubic volume that both connects
and separates the apartment's three
rooms. The screens open and close to

adapt to various situations and activities.
Allen explains that they were specifically
designed to facilitate different uses of the
space, with work in mind: 'The client was
keen on a completely open-plan scheme
to give a greater feeling of space. Since
he often works from home, he wanted to
be able to close the space off to provide
a quiet workplace; all of the screens,
therefore, are fitted with seals to ensure that
they acoustically separate the rooms.'

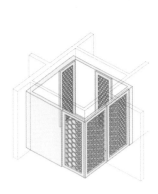

1 HALL / SCREEN
2 STUDY
3 KITCHEN AND LIVING ROOM
4 BEDROOM
5 BATHROOM

DOMESTIC FENCES

FUGA_OFFICINA DELL'ARCHITETTURA
MILAN, ITALY

For this family residence in Milan, the design scheme 'fences off' a number of private areas – bathroom, walk-in wardrobe, study – within an open space, so that they structure the rest of the flat and define other functions, including the living room, kitchen and two bedrooms. To reinforce this 'broken-plan' approach, architect Francesco Ursitti developed a series of angled doors, which pivot to form new spatial configurations that appear to continually reshape the apartment. The design carves out some additional space for the study niche, giving it back to the living room when the study is not in use. Ursitti, whose work is largely based on compositional experiments, used this project to rethink our experience of 'everyday spaces' through a simple device like a door – approached here as a means of creating 'hybrid spaces that are never complete'.

ILLUSTRATOR'S APARTMENT

CLAUDIA BRESCIANI & JÚLIA RISI
SÃO PAULO, BRAZIL

Brazilian architects Claudia Bresciani and Júlia Risi have refurbished a family apartment, which now includes an illustrator's studio. Simple finishing materials and a deliberately neutral environment are adapted to showcase the artworks and highlight the creative studio itself. A folding door of the kind that is normally found in industrial spaces has proven a practical and comfortable solution for this live–work arrangement. Made from translucent Plexiglas, it provides the necessary degree of privacy while maintaining a sense of connection with the rest of the house, without obstructing the light. Conveniently retracting upwards, the door leaves the floorspace unoccupied and completely opens the workspace into the living/dining room, which doubles as a gallery for the artist's graphic works.

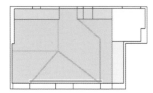

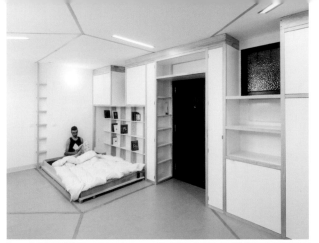

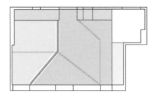

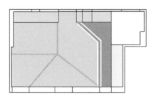

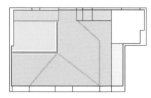

BIOMBOMBASTIC

ELII
MADRID, SPAIN

The design for this 25 m² (258 sq ft) studio flat in central Madrid is part of an experimental series in which ELII architects – Uriel Fogué, Eva Gil and Carlos Palacios – propose transformable spaces that turn an apartment into 'a small domestic theatre'. A large, two-fold screen wheels along the wooden rails to create a variety of arrangements – it can close off the bedroom or the kitchen, or simply divide the apartment in two. The upper part of the screen is made from transparent polycarbonate, which allows light into the partitioned space. When not in use, the screen is folded flat along one of the walls. Further 'stage equipment' for those 'experiments with oneself' includes a fold-out table and a pull-down bed with bookshelves concealed behind it. The kitchen, washing machine, other storage spaces and the bathroom door are built into the L-shaped functional 'band' that is articulated with wooden planks to match the structure of the screen and its guide rails.

DOMINO LOFT

PETER SUEN & CHARLES IRBY
SAN FRANCISCO, CALIFORNIA

Peter Suen and Charles Irby used concrete, steel and wooden slats to design a bespoke multifunctional structure that contains a dining room, full-size wardrobe, bedroom, guest bed and workspace for a young San Francisco-based couple. Taking advantage of the high floor-to-ceiling dimensions, the design team decided to treat this compact apartment as a loft, and defined a horizontal 'datum' with the 'sleep' area placed above it and the 'work' area below. 'In this manner, we have minimal moving elements (the main one being the folding bed that also functions as a dry-erase board), but the spaces are still multifunctional,' Suen comments, adding that such visual and physical separation between different functions helps their clients to 'develop a routine and a sense that the lower space is for work'.

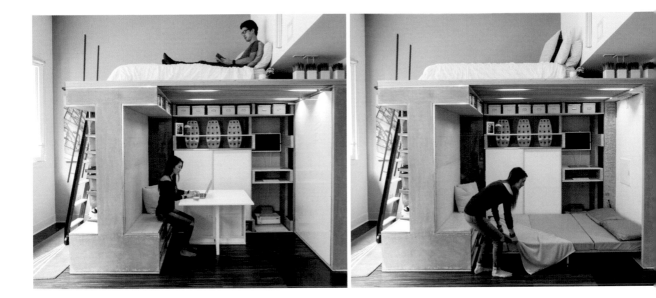

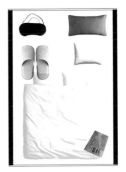

HOME & OFFICE

ROBERTO MONSANI & SILVIA ALLORI
FLORENCE, ITALY

This 1970s design by Roberto Monsani, the architect known for his human-centred, detail-conscious projects, so impressed Silvia Allori that she decided to make it both her home and office. She added a few new touches to the original design, including wooden flooring, neutral-coloured upholstery, and a golden curtain that separates the kitchen block from the entrance hall. The curtain is, in fact, a repurposed isothermal emergency blanket from a survival kit – one of the few eye-catchers brought into this rigidly structured space. Niches, as well as small and large steps, can accommodate sofas and beds. Most of the storage is concealed behind neat white laminate surfaces. The tabletop folds out of the storage wall and can be concealed to keep the room as uncluttered as possible, while neon lighting is hidden between the wall and its cladding. Walls feature a system of holes and pegs for hanging shelves – freely, but within the given grid.

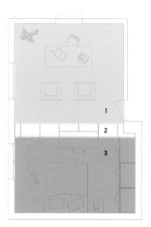

INHABITED
WOODEN WALLS

AURÉLIE MONET KASISI
GENEVA, SWITZERLAND

The owners of this residence in Geneva wanted to add storage space to two large rooms and divide them into four smaller ones, to host a home cinema, playroom, home office and bedroom for the au pair. Architect Aurélie Monet Kasisi designed a dividing wall with a number of integrated functions. In the first, full-height wall-to-wall shelving houses the family's media collection and integrates a small door leading to the playroom on the other side, with a circular opening that allows the parents to keep an inconspicuous eye on the children. In the second pair of rooms, the partition has office shelving on one side, and incorporates a fold-out desk for the au pair on the other. Both structures, along with other furniture and accessories designed for the rooms, were built from oiled pine plywood. The shelving rests on a series of supports made from recycled bricks and lawn-edging elements, and appears as decorative encrustation on the other side of the wall.

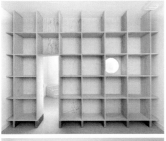

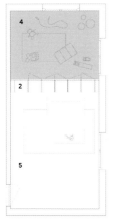

SUSALOON

ELII
MADRID, SPAIN

Madrid-based architectural collective ELII – an acronym for 'everyday life invents itself' – reconfigures and densifies an extended living room in the client's apartment to create a flexible space with multiple functions in a footprint of 23.5 m² (253 sq ft). This is achieved through a triple strategy of adapting the overall configuration of the apartment to the resident's lifestyle, removing unnecessary subdivisions – with an additional benefit of affording beautiful skyline views, and developing a series of fold-down furniture items and sliding panels. A workspace, a long dining table or a bed for a surprise guest can therefore be deployed as necessary, within the same room, while the sliding panels provide a temporary screen for privacy, then retract into the wall. When not in use, the furniture disappears within the built-in storage shelves on two sides of the room, leaving enough space for the owner to practise shiatsu or throw a party.

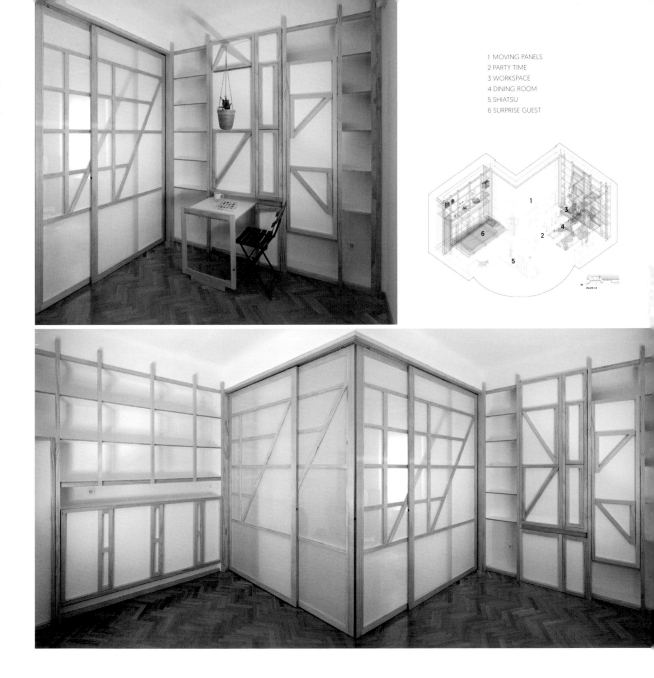

1 MOVING PANELS
2 PARTY TIME
3 WORKSPACE
4 DINING ROOM
5 SHIATSU
6 SURPRISE GUEST

HARRY

DIXNEUFCENTQUATREVINGTSIX
PARIS, FRANCE

Harry, the young owner of this attic apartment in Paris, has a total of 14 m² (151 sq ft) in which he wishes to 'conveniently eat, sleep, wash himself, entertain and work'. To make this possible, architects Mathilde Gaudemet and Arthur Ozenne have designed a built-in, full-height, L-shaped wall system that minimizes the need for additional furniture. With its minimalist, uniformly white exterior, this all-inclusive structure incorporates the 1 m × 2.2 m (3 ft 4 in. × 7 ft 3 in.) toilet/shower room on one side, while the other is shared between the kitchenette, wardrobe and workspace, which caters to Harry's work as a brand consultant and DJ. From under the 'office niche' – lined with acoustic foam for neighbour-friendly sound insulation – a couple of invisibly slotted chairs pull out to reveal a slide-out mixing desk.

COMPACT LIVING

SPACON & X
COPENHAGEN, DENMARK

Nikoline Dyrup Carlsen and Svend Jacob Pedersen, the duo behind Copenhagen-based studio Spacon & X and parents of two, remodelled their modest flat to suit the family's evolving needs. 'Instead of moving, we changed our way of thinking from square metres to cubic metres; from static rooms to flexible, activity-based zones,' they say. The scheme included a home office slotted between the living room and the children's domain. Concealed inside the wall, the 'cabinet-office' has a fold-down table and shelving with plug-in stools. It also stores a computer screen, printer, files and 'everything else one needs in a well-equipped office'. Its rear side doubles as a whiteboard, on which the couple sketch out their ideas. When stored away, the 'office' makes available a letterbox, as an alternative to having work papers scattered all around the place.

UNFOLDING
APARTMENT

MICHAEL K. CHEN ARCHITECTURE
NEW YORK, NEW YORK

In this 37.2 m² (400 sq ft) apartment, the client, a single young man, frequently entertains and occasionally works. In a reaction against 'the typical Manhattan approach of dividing a small space into even smaller individual rooms', here architect Michael K. Chen has developed a high-density scheme, in which numerous functional components – a bed with a nightstand, a wardrobe, a home office and library, as well as kitchen storage and most of the lighting – are fitted into a bespoke

bright-blue monolithic piece of furniture. A single pivoting panel provides a privacy screen for the bed, or forms an office nook with its fold-down desk, which can also be used for serving drinks at parties. A series of built-in aluminium billets placed at relevant heights act as grips and handles for manipulating the cabinet's doors and panels; lighting fixtures are invisibly integrated within the top of the cabinet to evenly illuminate the space.

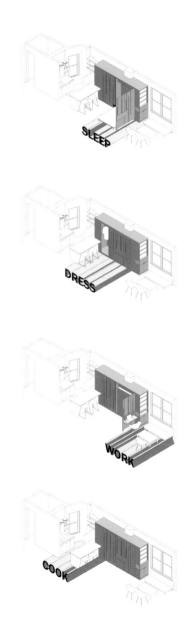

SLEEP

DRESS

WORK

COOK

ATTIC TRANSFORMER

MICHAEL K. CHEN ARCHITECTURE
NEW YORK, NEW YORK

Situated in an 1840s townhouse in New York's West Village, this 21 m² (226 sq ft) triple-aspect apartment was the smallest one that architect Michael K. Chen had ever dealt with – not to mention that it had never been renovated. The process of transforming this into an efficient and convenient home started with 'gutting the space to studs and rebuilding it from the inside out', as the architect puts it. The completely revised interior meets the challenge of 'maximizing space and function' with a degree of playfulness. A custom-built transformer block incorporates a series of roll-out features, including a clothing rack and a pantry, as well as a workstation with a separate plugged-in compartment to house the computer monitor. Besides a generously equipped micro-kitchen housing functions the owner never expected to have, one of the project's main highlights is the 1.8 m (5 ft 11 in.)-long tabletop that pulls out gradually as it evolves from a home office desk to a dining table, which – inconceivably for such a tiny space – seats up to five people.

ARTIST STUDIO

RUST ARCHITECTS
TEL AVIV, ISRAEL

Architects Raanan Stern and Shany Tal have fitted out a 20 m² (215 sq ft) studio within an artist's apartment. In addition to a workspace, the owner needed a storage system for a collection that consisted mostly of two-dimensional artworks, but also a dedicated space for materials and tools. To devise an efficient system for storing multiple objects of various sizes and uses, the design team spent a month measuring each object, and identified four different categories. Storage compartments with relevant proportions were developed for each category; the drawers' colour-coded sides help with recognition. Further compartments were adapted for storing work materials. The objects' accessibility has been calibrated according to their frequency of use, and smaller storage sections can be removed and placed on the work table as necessary. A sliding door doubles as a display board or an easel; when removed, it reveals a fold-down guest bed.

URBAN HERMITAGE

SPHERON ARCHITECTS
LONDON, UK

The name of the project, Urban Hermitage, reflects the client's vision for the studio flat, in which this London-based artist would work and practise yoga and meditation. On a surface of 26 m² (280 sq ft), Spheron Architects were requested to recreate 'the tranquil and melancholic beauty of a remote monastery in Belgium', undisturbed by the bustling city. An empty space with a simple table facing a bare concrete wall, dark wooden flooring and a white, light-diffusing curtain – the only soft element in the room – succeed in recreating the solitary, monastic ambience sought by the client. The scheme compresses the kitchen/bathroom and bedroom/wardrobe into two blocks and places them at opposite ends of the room. Wooden and mirror panelling renders these practicalities invisible, while at the same time making the studio appear open and spacious despite its modest size.

POCKETS

While some require a clearly articulated and sufficiently screened study, others prefer a more spontaneous, or 'scattered', arrangement. Still others need an easily transported or disassembled workspace for limited periods of time. This chapter explores how 'pop-up' and 'pocket' designs increase the capacity of a space to make it usable for homeworking, as well as other activities.

The description of Jonathan Olivares's hybrid of a lounge seat and pop-up workspace (pp. 178–9) as part of 'a new generation of products that cannot be classified by typology, because [they] can freely be used in multiple ways' applies to most of the projects and usage scenarios shown here. Ying Chang's Grid System (pp. 168–9), an average-sized table with a series of add-on accessories, has evolved from the designer's research into people's 'personal preferences towards their table', as she was not sure that the conventional form addressed the ways in which tables were used in a contemporary home. Chang's project, as well as Llot Llov's Clark Nude desk (p. 197), Line Depping's Borrod table (pp. 198–9) or Kentaro Yamazaki's Unfinished House (pp. 192–3), are designed to 'facilitate appropriation by the people who work and live' with them.

Work and leisure share the same territory – and the same kitchen-meets-study furniture – in Tenhachi architects' own family home in Japan (pp. 180–1), as well as in the apartment fitout for an urban couple in Austria by Kombinat architects (pp. 182–3). A champion of 'working wherever you want', Michael Hilgers has transformed an artist's easel into a pop-up workstation, to be deployed with equal ease in a bedroom or a garden [p. 170]. For a few years, an attic will be the personal space of a family's growing son, for whom architect Stefano Viganò crafted a compact multipurpose device that fuses a desk, a bed and a storage system [pp. 188–9]. ENORME Studio have hacked Ikea items to create a temporary study, bedroom and storage area for a young researcher returning from abroad and staying in her two brothers' shared living room [pp. 186–7]. Note Design Studio outfitted the main living space of a loft so that it could be used both for friendly gatherings and receiving international business clients [pp. 194–5].

Architect Ben Allen [whose designs are presented in earlier chapters] is specifically interested in 'the breakdown of barriers between work and home'. His firm's residential projects seek to create spaces in which 'everything from the kitchen table to an armchair to a window seat to a proper desk area is envisaged to be used for working of some sort'. This, Allen notes, responds to the open-plan nature of many living spaces, but also to the reality of a family home, in which 'degrees of activity or noise may vary, so there are times when retreating to a corner is preferable and times when the main space in the house would be ideal'.

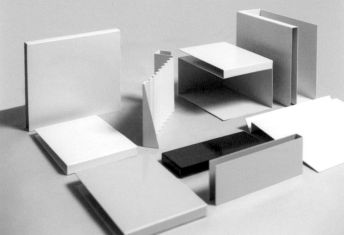

GRID SYSTEM

YING CHANG

London-based designer Ying Chang proposes a dynamic three-dimensional alternative to a traditional table. 'As our living spaces continue to shrink, the distinction between a table and a desk gets blurred,' she explains. 'A table has become a multitasking surface. Smaller amounts of space are needed for the many different tasks it performs.' Central to her project is the grid system, valued by architects and graphic designers for its capacity to impose order and at the same time foster versatility in terms of use. A tubular metal frame supports a vast array of accessories that can be added and removed to adapt to the user's needs. These include three kinds of boxes formed from steel mesh, coloured shelves of folded aluminium sheets, as well as trays in wood, concrete and other materials.

HIDESK

MICHAEL HILGERS
MUELLERMOEBEL.DE

Developed with a view to the paperless office gradually becoming a reality, the collapsible HIDEsk is a pop-up workspace for urban micro-flats, but can also be used for occasional work on a balcony or in the garden. 'As small as possible, as big as necessary,' as designer Michael Hilgers puts it, HIDEsk is in fact an artist's easel remade into a portable study for a laptop worker. Three acrylic trays plug into perforated slots to provide minimal storage space and support a digital tablet. When completely folded, the desk occupies virtually no space, while its front side – optionally coated with blackboard paint – can be used as a board for memos or sketches.

JOY ZETA

ARCO DESIGN STUDIO
ARCO.NL

Created by the in-house design team of
Dutch furniture manufacturer Arco, this
space-efficient, wall-leaning desk is sized
for a modern, laptop-reliant home office.
The use of solid wood and the rounded
edges and joints allow the workspace to
blend into the domestic interior. A groove

in the tabletop provides storage for small
objects and has an opening for cables.
Here, the desk has been accessorized with
a Cable Sock; this 3D-knitted 'stocking' by
designer Jonathan Prestwich conceals the
cables and routes them down the table leg
in an orderly but playful manner.

PUZZLE WALL

SPACON & X

Conceived by the Danish design duo Spacon & X, Puzzle Wall enhances the capacity of domestic furniture to adapt to residents' evolving needs. Those might be long term (a growing family, or changes in style of living or working), or short term (having to switch between 'home', 'work' and 'party' mode in the space of a few hours). Puzzle Wall enables the set up of a permanent or collapsible home office whose configuration can vary from 'a small standing workspot in the living room to a bigger meeting table'. When friends come over, the table can be moved along the wall or folded away. Slot-in shelves in perforated steel can also function as memo boards. Benches and stools are plugged on to plywood 'box shelves' for elegant, zero-space storage.

HOME BACK HOME: CASE STUDY #01 DUNE CLAUDIO

PKMN ARCHITECTURES
MADRID, SPAIN

This project is part of the Home Back Home series of case studies, in which the Spanish collective PKMN (now ENORME Studio and EEESTUDIO) have developed pop-up live–work solutions for young people who had to temporarily return to their parents' homes. Having moved back to her 9 m² (97 sq ft) teenage bedroom, fashion and leather technician and textile artist Dune Claudio decided that this could be an opportunity to dedicate more time to her personal fashion design projects. Obliged to keep the existing furniture, Dune needed a solution for fitting a fully equipped workstation into the extremely tight space that remained. A number of brainstorming sessions with PKMN, in which Dune has participated as a co-designer, resulted in a lightweight, knock-down system built with recycled parts of her old bookcase and desk. The structure integrates two fold-down work surfaces for designing and sewing, a set of sliding storage boxes for tools and materials, a lamp with a witty adjustment mechanism, and even a space for the tailor's dummy.

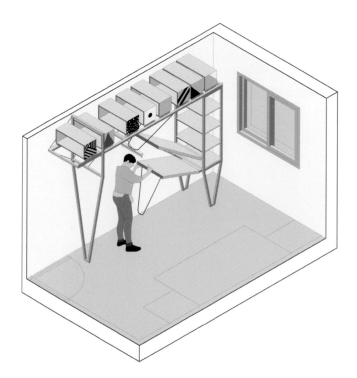

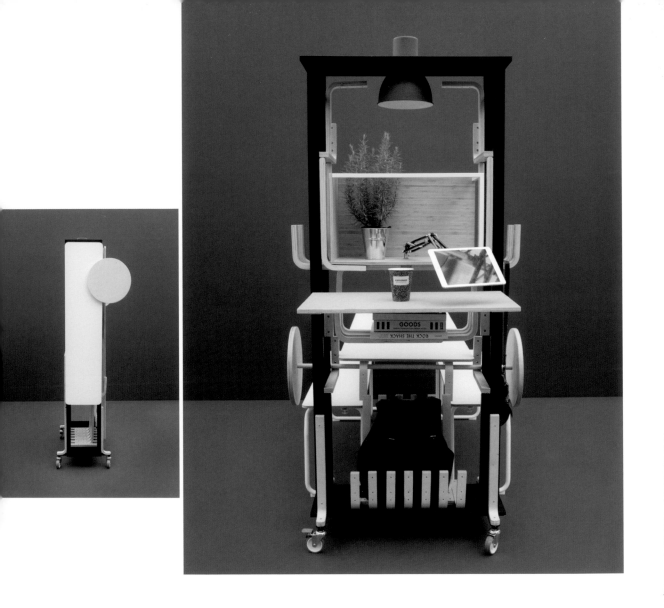

IKEA HACK

SPACON & X

As participants in Ikea's Space10 laboratory, dedicated to 'exploring new ways of future living', the designers at Spacon & X have deconstructed a few of Ikea's pieces, reusing the components in their multipurpose scheme for small-space urban living. With flexibility and transformation being key to Spacon & X's designs, Ikea Hack is compact when folded, moves on castors and integrates – from top to bottom – a lamp, a box shelf with an articulating tablet holder, a pull-up standing desk with additional storage behind it, and a bag shelf. An 'eat-meet-read' table flaps out on the other side and is complemented by two folding benches, which are hooked to the lateral walls when not needed. The hooks themselves can also be used for hanging clothes, bags or as an occasional magazine rack.

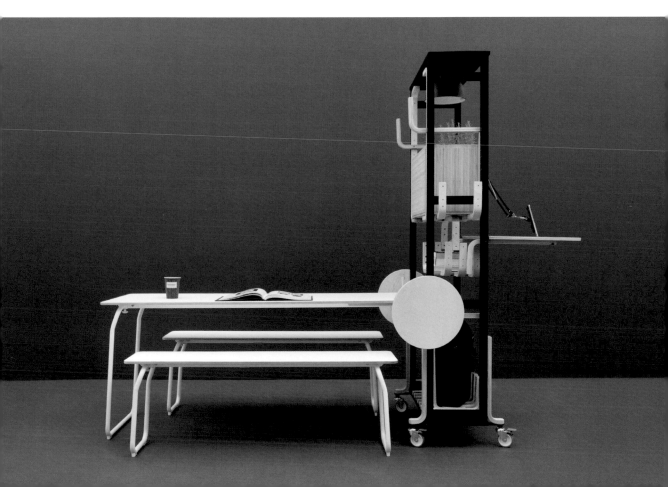

TERRITORIO

JONATHAN OLIVARES
DANESE.COM

Wide enough to accommodate your laptop, your food, your reading matter and so on, Territorio is at once a seat and a work area. US-based designer Jonathan Olivares intended it as a means to create one's own 'privacy island' within a larger space. An extra-large seat measuring 120 × 85 cm (3 ft 11 in. × 2 ft 9 in.) combined with the absence of a physical enclosure lets the user define their personal space, yet they are able to engage with what is going on around them.

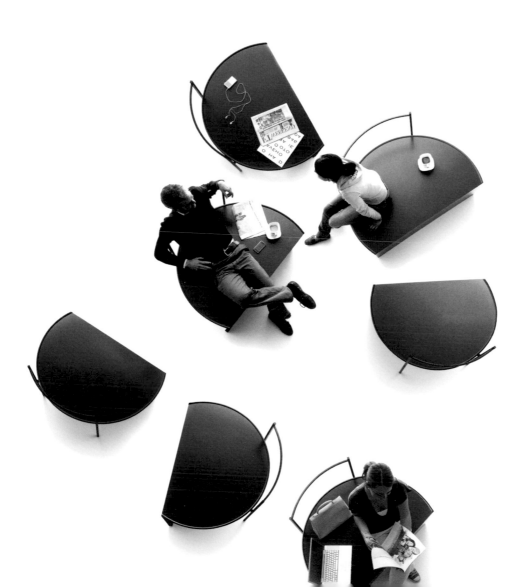

TENHACHI HOUSE

TENHACHI
TOKYO, JAPAN

Tomoko Sasaki and Kei Sato, the principals at the Japanese architectural firm Tenhachi, have reconfigured their 67 m² [721 sq ft] flat to reflect their concept of a home as a combination of 'public and private behaviours'. The single-space scheme with two box-like volumes that house the master bedroom and the bathroom creates a sense of openness; only the toilet is hidden. The top of the bedroom box acts as the children's playroom. Positioned close to the entrance, the boxes open into the main living area, which receives generous amounts of daylight and is dominated by a 4.5 m [14 ft 9 in.]-long multipurpose table. This table incorporates the kitchen and the bookshelf, hosts family meals and accommodates up to 20 guests, but also serves as a workstation for the parents and a desk for the kids. The idea of a house in which everything is 'gently connected' is therefore faithfully maintained at all scales.

APARTMENT AB

KOMBINAT
VIENNA, AUSTRIA

'Rather than separating work from leisure, the apartment enables both activities to be performed in the same space, and at the same time.' This was the concept put forward by the Slovenian architectural firm Kombinat for their clients in Vienna, a couple that 'lives and breathes urban life'. The design team removed two partition walls and restored the typical layout of an old bourgeois apartment in which the living room faces the street, while the bedrooms are oriented towards the courtyard. This has allowed them to create a spacious 'public area' with a long table for hosting 'lunches, work-related meetings or both at once'. Another key element of this multipurpose room is a wall-to-wall counter that stretches along the street-facing windows to integrate a kitchen, a desk and a seating nook. Reflecting the couple's lifestyle, 'work and leisure are intertwined and mix constantly, while none of the elements dominates', the clients comment. On top of that, the library with a desk and a couch offers an alternative, more intimate work environment.

1 KITCHEN + LIVING/DINING ROOM + WORKSPACE
2 LIBRARY + COUCH
3 BEDROOM
4 ENTRANCE HALL
5 BATHROOM

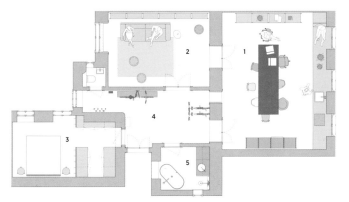

MICRO-APARTMENT MOABIT

SPAMROOM & JOHN PAUL COSS
BERLIN, GERMANY

Originally, this 21 m² (226 sq ft) flat in a 1900s residential building in Berlin had a shared toilet in an outbuilding downstairs. A private bathroom added by the previous owner had improved the comfort but unbalanced the overall set up of an already tiny space. In their renovation scheme, architects Paola Bagna (spamroom) and John Paul Coss chose to remove all the interior walls and appropriate the studio's entire volume as a means to declutter the floor plan while 'maximizing the potential of every centimetre'. Considerable ceiling height allowed for a bathroom box with enough space on top to host a sleeping deck with a book- and laptop shelf. The kitchen and storage block wraps around the bathroom's outer wall; the thin yet robust steel staircase gives access to both the bedroom and the full-height wardrobe, while an extended window sill acts as a desk.

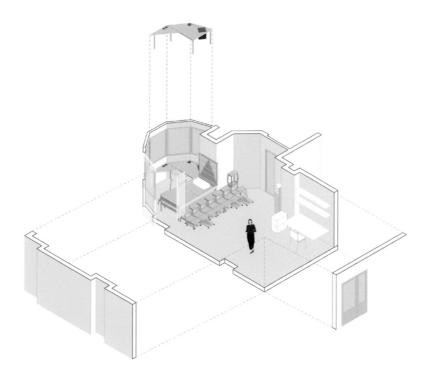

HOME BACK HOME: CASE STUDY #03 ANA MOMBIEDRO

ENORME STUDIO
MADRID, SPAIN

In another project from the Home Back Home series (see also pp. 174–5), the team at ENORME Studio looked at the case of Ana Mombiedro, who had returned to Spain after a series of research visits to finish her PhD thesis in her two brothers' shared home. With no space available for a private room, Ana was offered the bay window area in the living room, which her brothers used for both work and leisure activities. The challenge, say the architects, was to arrange in the alcove a pop-up bedroom and study without compromising the social nature of the apartment's main

communal area. Their workshop was sponsored by Ikea, so the team could customize several of the brand's products. Placed in the room's best-lit area, the shape of the desk was adapted to the configuration of the window. The bed could close like a box during the day and flap open at night, exposing extra features such as integrated lighting and occasional book supports. Finally, a two-level installation composed of some 16 wooden stools formed storage for books, plants and Ana's shoes, which are placed on rolling trays.

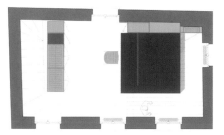

THE ROOM
FOR GIÒ

STEFANO VIGANÒ
SONDRIO, ITALY

The family for which Stefano Viganò had once renovated this residence in the Italian town of Sondrio called him back, as their son Giò had grown up. The architect was asked to revisit the attic – a 25 m² (269 sq ft) space with two outdoor terraces on opposite sides – and convert it into the teenager's own private room. He started by painting the ceiling and three walls white; this made the room considerably brighter and helped to highlight a beautiful structural element: the massive, solid wood roof truss. The open plan was retained, with the entire live–study–play programme consolidated within a single elevated platform with a low divider separating the desk from the sleeping and relaxation area. The platform is essentially a big white block with assorted wooden panels on top. Four panels lift to uncover the bed; others conceal storage for clothes, books, games and Giò's other belongings.

RENOVATION
IN BRIXEN

PHILIPP KAMMERER & MARTIN EGGER
BRIXEN/BRESSANONE, ITALY

The owners of this two-storey attic apartment wished to upgrade it with a flexible extra space that could serve as a guest room or a study, complete with a number of storage options. The property is located in a densely built residential complex, and so architects Philipp Kammerer and Martin Egger took special care to retain as much of the existing roof structure as possible; privacy was another concern they had to deal with.

The resulting space locks into the L-shaped upper floor and connects to the existing open-plan living room. The new access door is the extension's only opening to the outside – except, of course, for the patio, which hosts a tree and brings daylight to this part of the house. Built from prefabricated timber elements, the structure integrates a storage wall on one side, while the other side is open to various uses and currently serves as a home office.

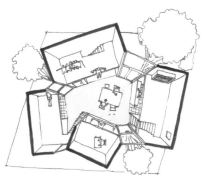

UNFINISHED HOUSE

YAMAZAKI KENTARO DESIGN WORKSHOP
KASHIWA, JAPAN

Being a co-designer of your house, making changes as you are living in it, is both a challenge and a continued pleasure, believes architect Kentaro Yamazaki. His 'long, fruitful discussions with the client' gave shape to a project that offers its residents exactly this opportunity. Four box-like volumes, each containing two floors, surround the central, double-height atrium that serves as a living/dining room and a 'family hub'. The boxes' lower levels accommodate the kitchen, bedroom, bathroom and workroom. The upper-floor spaces have been intentionally left blank, Yamazaki explains, so the family can adapt them to their changing hobbies, growing wardrobes, working needs and, specifically, to allow the children to be creative in fitting out their own rooms. All boxes are oriented for optimal exterior views; the position of the kitchen box facilitates keeping an eye on the kids.

INNER CITY BLUE

NOTE DESIGN STUDIO
STOCKHOLM, SWEDEN

The first private residence outfitted by Note Design Studio happened to be for a senior executive of a large company who was also a board member for a few others. She worked from her office and from home and wanted to be able to receive Swedish and international business clients in her family apartment. In other words, the communal spaces in this 200 m² (2,153 sq ft) Stockholm loft had to be relaxed, but also elaborately elegant, as a kind of international and timeless 'salon'.

To achieve the desired mood, the designers removed the excesses that remained from previous renovations and put together a 'soft and hazy' palette that used no white. Initially regarded as a problem, the client's request for ample storage in a loft with mostly sloping walls finally provided the organizational basis for the entire project. Low but deep cabinets form a blue-grey band that wraps around the loft 'like a unifying horizon ... for the ceiling height to shoot off'.

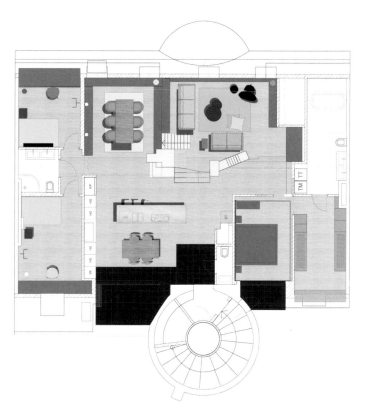

BALKONZEPT

MICHAEL HILGERS
REPHORM.DE

BalKonzept is part of German designer Michael Hilgers's growing collection of products that cater to contemporary urbanites, their shrinking homes and their mobile, laptop-sized workspaces. It simply hooks on to balcony railings to serve as a pop-up open-air office, and can then switch its function to become a lunch table or bar. The recessed planter in the upper part of the 'balcony desk' can also be used as a cooler for drinks, or as occasional storage for magazines and other items.

CLARK NUDE

LLOT LLOV
LLOTLLOV.DE

For those homeworkers who have not yet reached the paperless stage, Berlin-based collective Llot Llov have designed a desk that puts paper mess out of sight without entirely removing it from view and therefore from memory, as is often the case with traditional drawers. Having observed that the stacks of papers that tend to accumulate on desks seem chaotic but in fact have their own hidden order, the designers vowed to find a better way to handle those stacks, before they completely submerge the work surface. Their Clark Nude desk accomplishes this through a series of 'pockets' and recesses. A shallower recess at the rear contains the stationery; a deep 'pocket' to the left is suited to box files; while another one, open on two sides, holds those notorious stacks of papers and magazines. The pockets are set flush with the desk and slightly tilted towards it, which makes their contents easy to reach while keeping the workspace reasonably tidy.

BORROD

LINE DEPPING

Danish designer Line Depping focuses on situations, behaviours and usage patterns rather than objects as such, and this is why her projects often involve movement and change. With her Borrod table, which is equally well suited to working, dining and playing, mess is not a problem, Depping says. When the time comes to switch from one activity to another, the two halves of the tabletop pull apart to reveal a robust textile pocket hidden below, allowing for a quick and easy clean-up.

TATSUMI APARTMENT HOUSE

HIROYUKI ITO ARCHITECTS
TOKYO, JAPAN

The location of this ten-storey residential tower – close to heavy traffic and above a subway station – required a reinforced concrete structure with massive columns and beams. But how to mitigate their presence in a modest 34 m² (366 sq ft) apartment? Architect Hiroyuki Ito's solution consisted of designing multipurpose sunken floors and alcoves. As the structural elements become progressively more slender towards the higher floors, this 'functional landscape' varies from floor to floor. On the lower storeys, thick beams create a considerable drop in floor height, which is interpreted as a tier-like bench, a recessed lounge pad or a place for built-in storage, while spacious window niches produced by the columns integrate kitchen blocks, working desks or seating nooks – sometimes in two-in-one configurations. On the top floor, the 'landscape' flattens, offering full-height window views instead.

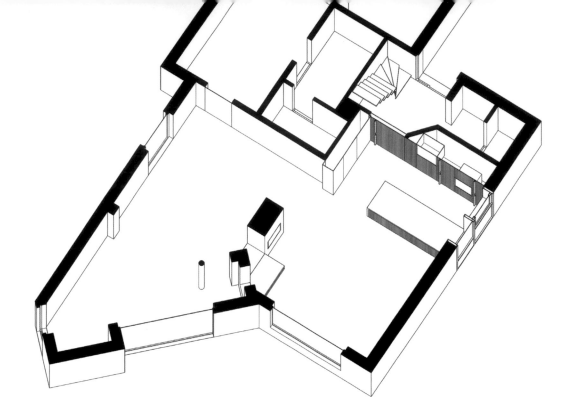

HOUSE S&J

MAF ARCHITECTEN
BEERNEM, BELGIUM

Belgian studio Maf Architecten merged a study with a living room for a couple who 'wanted to spend time together, but found themselves either separated from each other or improvising an office space on the dining table'. Initially, the clients wanted to create a window-like opening between the living room and the adjacent study, but the architects proposed a more radical move and tore the wall down to create a layout in which the two spaces would enhance each other. The home office is now in a pocket-like niche that opens into the living room. A desk is integrated into a new, custom-built window structure, so the workspace receives enough natural light. Behind the table, a bespoke wall cabinet provides storage for the office and separates the living room from the entrance hall. The veneered panelling echoes the antique wooden furniture in the living room, two glazed niches display the family's valuables, and the desk itself serves as a bar during parties.

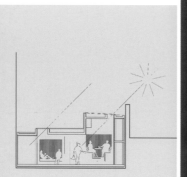

SAINT LOUIS HOUSE

CHRISTIAN POTTGIESSER
ARCHITECTURESPOSSIBLES
PARIS, FRANCE

Squeezed between the three neighbours' walls, this micro-house in a Parisian courtyard occupies a niche that is 8.8 m (28 ft 10 in.) long and 4 m (13 ft) deep. Architect Christian Pottgiesser has carefully balanced the owners' hospitality with their need for privacy by surrounding the multipurpose central space – open towards the outside and abundantly lit through the glazed façade with a pivoting entrance door – with a thick 'service wall'

that conceals the bed-sized bedroom, as well as the bathroom and the kitchen. To keep the main space uncluttered, two alcoves are incorporated into the same wall: one is a seating nook complete with a bookcase, while the other is a hybrid of a study and a dining room. Additional cantilevered seats slide out and retract to accommodate guests, and also serve as steps that eventually lead to the hidden sleeping deck overhead.

GM APARTMENT

ONSIDE ARCHITECTURE
VALENCIA, SPAIN

Spanish architecture firm Onside have renovated an apartment for a family of five. The residence needed revamping to remedy several problems: insufficient storage; dark, poorly ventilated spaces; incoherent design; and a messy 'mixture of uses'. In addition, each family member needed his or her own workspace. The new layout, with its unified material palette, is organized around a line of storage cabinets and wardrobes that double as dividers between the now better-connected spaces. The three children's workstations were placed in their rooms, but the parents' office proved trickier to locate. Rather than opting for a 'conservative' solution, such as a separate monofunctional room, the team situated it in the evenly lit corridor. Set within the service and storage wall, this 'office alcove' has the triple advantage of not reducing the size of other rooms; having enough shelving space close at hand; and receiving natural light from the window.

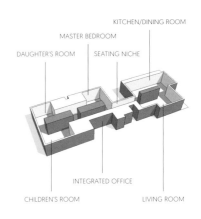

KITCHEN/DINING ROOM

MASTER BEDROOM

DAUGHTER'S ROOM   SEATING NICHE

INTEGRATED OFFICE

CHILDREN'S ROOM   LIVING ROOM

DATUM HOUSE

ROB KENNON ARCHITECTS
MELBOURNE, AUSTRALIA

In this restored and expanded house, architect Rob Kennon used volume and light as his primary means for defining various functional zones. The distinct 'datum line' traced throughout the building highlights the differently treated roof shapes in the adjacent areas. This means that while the living room has a gabled, 'cathedral-like' ceiling, the monopitched roof in the kitchen/dining room rises from the datum line to allow the morning sun through the clerestory windows on the opposite wall. 'The clients wanted a design that would encourage interaction, but would also provide some relief for parents when needed,' the design team explain. In addition to a separate study, the dining room incorporates two alcoves – one occupied by the kitchen, and the other by a craft desk for the clients' two daughters 'to play and create ... the parents can observe and join in as they go about their daily activities'.

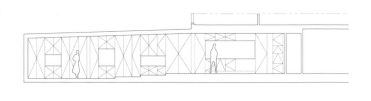

JM HOUSE

ATELIER VAN WENGERDEN
AMSTERDAM, NETHERLANDS

For the rather typical situation of a growing family that needs more living space without moving away from the dynamic urban area where it currently dwells, architect Jacco van Wengerden has designed what he describes as 'a sensitive extension'. The scheme doubles the living space, but also enhances contact with the outdoors. The key to this idea is an expanded kitchen that morphs into a corridor leading from the existing residence to the new extension.

The passage progresses in long, gradually descending steps slightly recessed into the ground. This heightens the sense of space, and the movement ends with an elevated outdoor terrace. While the corridor's garden-facing wall is entirely glazed, the other wall is transformed into a smart wooden cabinet 'that supplies and hides various functions' – including a series of plywood-framed niches for play and work.

STEPPED HOUSE

ROB KENNON ARCHITECTS
SYDNEY, AUSTRALIA

In a green suburb of Sydney, architect Rob Kennon and his team have designed this landscape-sensitive, south-facing addition to an Edwardian duplex house. The extension's façade is clad in local, weather-resistant timber, with the variously sized windows responding to both the exterior views and the degree of privacy desired by the residents. The master bedroom suite occupies the upper level; on the ground floor, a range of stepped platforms descends with the sloping topography,

effectively embedding the house in the landscape. Each platform defines a different functional zone – kitchen, dining room, lounge – within an open-plan layout. The staircase acts as a node that connects the different floors, as well as the old and new structures. Along the way, it forms an intimate 'pocket' that accommodates the study, while the exposed oak framing creates display shelves for both the study nook and the hallway.

This final chapter deals with workspaces that either completely merge with the architectural elements of the house – be it a staircase (p. 218) or a structural frame (pp. 220–1) – or branch off to form extensions or even detached backyard offices. An intermediate solution is a 'room within a room', which can be as small as an enclosed desk (pp. 230–1) or as big as a two-storey house within a painter's studio (pp. 224–5), which, additionally, inverts the traditional workspace/living space rapport.

The very nature of the task that requires privacy on one hand and organic inclusion in the domestic interior on the other often leads to designs that are at once integrated and detached. Take Shinichi Ogawa's design for a residence in Japan that incorporates an office into a minimalist family home while retaining its independence (pp. 226–7), or a home for two illustrators by Israeli architecture firm RUST, with their individual workstations placed in an acoustically protected glass box on the border between the apartment's private and communal areas (pp. 236–7).

From here, homeworking still has plenty of room to evolve. Convinced that designers should think a few years ahead, architect Rianne Makkink looks at the possibility of going from an individual workspace used by family members to housing projects that come complete with a co-working space for residents. 'I see working at home as working at home within a community,' she says. Makkink cites a practice that exists in some Nordic countries in which condominiums include independent guest rooms available to every resident. Why not develop similar solutions for workspaces, from shared desk space to a shared workshop?

Some of Makkink's colleagues think along similar lines. Thus, Boskop architects' design for 55 homes in Nantes, France, provides a shared 'plus-room' that can be connected, as needed, to any of three adjacent homes. For another French city, Montpellier, architecture firm Archikubik designed a public housing block with a separate 'extra room' on each floor, capable of accommodating a homeworker's office, a student room, and so on. The recently completed House for Seven People in Tokyo has its ground-floor space designed as a combination of a living room, café, library and workshop, which opens to the street and thus to other people who work and study in the neighbourhood. The architects, Mio Tsuneyama and Madeleine Kessler of Studio mnm, see this project as a catalyst for revival of the disappearing local community.

The chapter ends with a co-living and co-working project slated for a location in the Indian Himalayas (pp. 264–5). A stable high-speed Internet connection is crucial, enabling a retreat in 'one of the planet's most remote and beautiful corners' while allowing occupants to remain in touch with the wider world. That's just a hint at how detached and yet how integrated a homeworker can be right now.

OBJET ÉLEVÉ

STUDIO MIEKE MEIJER

Commissioned by interior designer Just Haasnoot for his own home, Objet Élevé is both an artwork and a multifunctional object that is at once a staircase, a shelving unit, and a workspace complete with a cabinet. Similar to other designs by the Dutch design duo of Mieke Meijer and Roy Letterlé, it is inspired by old industrial facilities, as seen in the black and white photos of Bernd and Hilla Becher. Partly suspended, partly floor-standing, the feature is defined by an exposed, three-dimensional steel frame with oak panels serving as treads, shelves and the desktop. Samba-style steps enable a compact structure with steep but convenient stairs, while at the same time articulating the black framework.

FLEXIT

PIETER PEULEN

Belgian designer Pieter Peulen's tribute to his years spent in a student residence, Flexit is a solution to add comfort to those 'small, hard to personalize and not flexible' rooms. The unit takes 20 minutes to assemble and consists of a pair of three-dimensional metal frames that are set on castors and support a standard-sized board to function as a desk or a bed. The two frames, each weighing about 8 kg (18 lbs), can be fastened together or stand alone. A nightstand, a shelf, a mirror and a basket can be clipped on as required. Needless to say, the frame offers multiple clothes-hanging possibilities, making it a rather ordered mess.

GEO METRIA

MOUNT FUJI ARCHITECTS
ODAWARA, JAPAN

It was a 'perfect living environment quietly waiting to be found', architects Masahiro and Mao Harada say about the site for this residence, a south-facing slope on a wooded hillside, sheltered from north winds and offering a distant sea view. Rather than going for a more traditional scheme, they have devised the project's shape by 'observing the site closely and finding its hidden geometry' in order to reflect and amplify its essential qualities.

The outcome is a building whose transparent front part exposes two sets of portal frames in laminated veneer lumber; intersecting at a certain angle, they echo the curved topography and prevent the long beams from sagging. As well as serving as the building's structural frame, the system acts as an unobtrusive room divider for the main, open-plan space and integrates shelving, as well as a study desk with a view.

1 FAMILY HOUSE
2 A1 STUDIO
3 PATIO
4 MEETING ROOM
5 TERRACE
6 TEAHOUSE
7 GARAGE + STORAGE

A1 HOUSE

A1 ARCHITECTS
PRAGUE, CZECH REPUBLIC

Architects David Maštálka and Lenka Křemenová, partners in life and work, cross-linked their home and office, as well as architecture old and new, in an area of Prague that retains its village-like character, despite being within walking distance of an underground station. The existing stone house and the new timber structure with a gabled roof and charred black façade intersect to form a symmetrical, cross-shaped plan. The old house accommodates the residential part, while the new addition contains the architecture office, with the degree of connection between the family space and the studio carefully measured. At the intersection of the two structures, the entrance hall (above, left) separates the home and work areas. The meeting room (above, right) is housed in a former shed located on the other side of the private garden from the studio. The kitchen has become the heart of the house, and is the place where the two realms converge.

HOUSE FOR A PAINTER

PRICEGORE
LONDON, UK

The former warehouse in which a painter had arranged his studio and an ad hoc residence for himself and his wife had to be remodelled to make a clearer distinction between 'home' and 'work' areas, as the couple were expecting their first child. London-based architects Pricegore's scheme for this double-height space was to transform an existing mezzanine into a two-storey house that occupied half of the industrial building inside which it sat. The house's front façade overlooks the studio space, making it appear as 'a small piazza or garden, a feeling further enhanced by the large landscape paintings in progress', Dingle Price notes. With the painter's plans to move to a new studio in the future, the workspace, which already comprises a kitchen/dining area, should become a 'grand living room', he adds.

F RESIDENCE

SHINICHI OGAWA & ASSOCIATES
GIFU, JAPAN

Architect Shinichi Ogawa has designed a glass house sandwiched between two slabs and 'floating in the middle of a vast rice field', for a family with two teenage sons. The house enjoys a 360° view of the natural scenery, with its immediate surroundings evolving from calm water to an expanse of tall rice shoots over the course of the year; a strip-like concrete bridge connects it to the road. Comprising 'home' and 'work' functions, the project

groups the living, kitchen and dining rooms and the office in its south-facing front part. The master bedroom and the boys' rooms – screened off by a utility core with incorporated private courtyards for the bathroom and toilet – are located at the rear. A perimetral outdoor terrace allows for separate entrances to the residence and the office, with the latter being separated from the living room by a double-sided storage/media/service wall.

SS GARDEN PAVILION

DE MEESTER VLIEGEN
ANTWERP, BELGIUM

An inscrutable black glass and polished concrete exterior conceals an entirely oak-clad interior, intended to instil an instant sense of calmness and warmth. This is part of the design scenario developed by De Meester Vliegen architects for the client, who needed a garden pavilion with a fully functioning office space that could also be used as a weekend guesthouse. Similar to the SS Penthouse (pp. 132–3), and designed by the same team for the same family, the interior had to feel like a living room rather than a regular office – hence the use of natural materials, warm colours, highlighted wood-grain texture and even a sitting area with a fireplace as part of the meeting room fitout. Utilities such as the kitchen, toilet and bathroom are seamlessly concealed behind massive wood panelling; full-height windows open on a walled garden with a row of trees that obscure the house to enhance privacy.

DIAPOSITIVE

RONAN & ERWAN BOUROULLEC
GLASITALIA.COM

The Bouroullec brothers champion flexible spaces with fewer walls, which can easily adapt to growing or shrinking families and changing life patterns. They seek to provide such spaces with 'universal objects' compatible with different kinds of settings. Many of these are intended as space-making furniture, like this series of alcove desks in coloured, thermo-welded glass, matched with similarly designed sofas, benches and shelves. Wooden edging protects the supporting panels and reduces any coldness or fragility associated with glass furniture; other accessories include cosy felt mats for seating and wooden panels to be laid on the desktop.

KOLORO DESK

TORAFU ARCHITECTS
ICHIRODESIGN.JP

Koloro is a playfully designed desk that defines its own privacy zone. It provides a solution for open-plan domestic interiors in which a homeworker may need a moment of calm and concentration. Japanese collective Torafu have developed Koloro – basically, a large but lightweight box on trestles – as a piece of micro-architecture, with its own skylight and windows that open as necessary, while their pull-down hatches function as shelves. The material, polyester-coated plywood, comes in a number of colours to create various 'environments' inside this room-in-a-room workspace. The seat of the Koloro stool conceals a storage compartment.

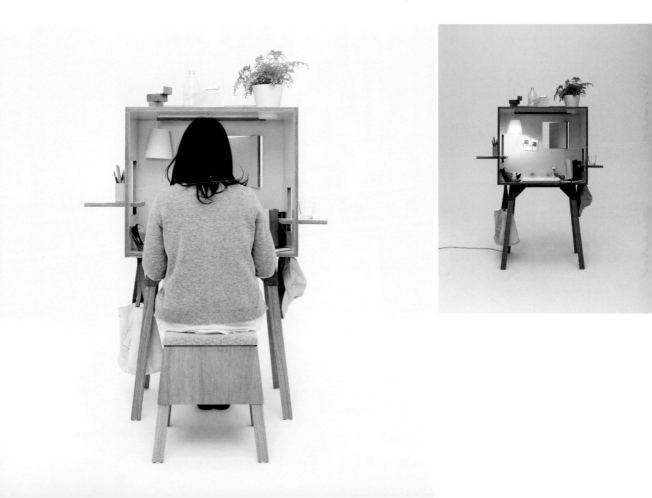

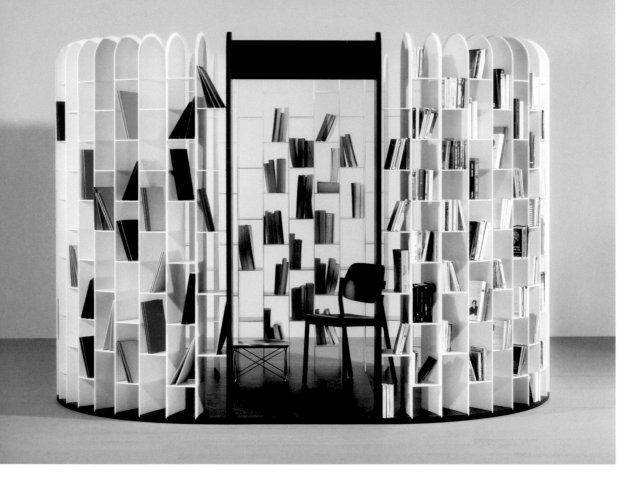

AREA, BLOCK

GILLES BELLEY

Area (above and opposite, bottom left and right) from Gilles Belley's conceptual series Room (see also p. 119) creates an enclosed place for concentrated work, reading or simply having a conversation inside a larger room. Its modular design can form a freestanding unit or adjoin a wall; depending on the position of the slots in Area's floor, the blade-like uprights can support bookshelves or be joined into an opaque screen. With Block (opposite, top left and right), the French designer attempts to condense the essential elements of a living space so that several functions – study, storage wall and bedroom – overlap within a single piece of furniture.

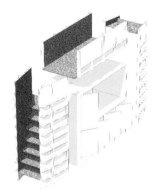

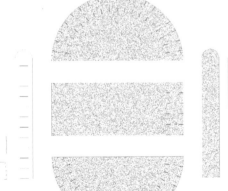

LIVING CUBE

TILL KÖNNEKER & DANA LOFTUS
LIVINGCUBE.FURNITURE

An original idea from the Swiss artist Till Könneker, developed further by Dana Loftus, the Living Cube consolidates up to twelve different furniture items in one small footprint, its creators explain. Initially Könneker developed the piece for his loft apartment in order to save on the time and cost of purchasing numerous furnishings to store his books, records, clothes, shoes, TV and DVDs, plus an extra bed for an occasional guest. His other concern was about the space these items would take up. The Living Cube addressed all those challenges at once, as it merged several storage units into one, but it also created an enclosure for an extra room and a sleeping deck on top. Today, the design includes a fold-down workspace and is available in a single-wall configuration. 'Additionally, the "new room" inside all Living Cubes can be customized as a pocket home office,' Loftus notes.

WORK AND LIVE

RUST ARCHITECTS
TEL AVIV, ISRAEL

RUST architects have remodelled this
53 m² (570 sq ft) flat for a young couple
working from home. Both are illustrators,
and each needs a personal workspace
isolated from the rest of the house. Having
divided the apartment into two zones –
private (bedroom, bathroom, wardrobe)
and communal (kitchen, living room and
dining room) – the design team placed
a transparent enclosure between them
for two workstations. Its simple iron frame

integrates a double-face cabinet, custom-
designed like all the other storage in this
project. The cabinet combines workspace
shelving and a media wall for the living
room; it also contains all of the apartment's
control systems. To enable parallel use of
home and work areas, acoustic comfort
was made a priority, notes RUST's Raanan
Stern. The project therefore uses double-
layer timber floors, insulated walls, and
acoustic tiles for the workspace ceiling.

1 LIVING ROOM
2 TWO STUDIOS
3 BEDROOM
4 KITCHEN/DINING ROOM
5 BATHROOM

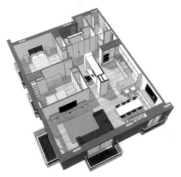

ARTILLERY MANSIONS

FORMSTUDIO
LONDON, UK

Architects FORMstudio have reimagined a typical developer flat layout to make use of the wasted internal corridor and create a more flexible, enjoyable and better-lit home. A crucial space-defining element has been introduced to the newly formed open-plan zone. This centrally positioned block conceals an existing structural column and houses a home office workstation. It also offers an elegant, functionally driven response to fire safety

regulations. The home office block screens off the kitchen to provide an escape route from the bedrooms and living space in case of fire, and incorporates concealed fire doors on electromagnetic holds. Besides protecting the escape route, these doors can be used to separate work and living areas, or to seal off the bedrooms from the living and cooking area.

WHITE ON WHITE

GIANNI BOTSFORD ARCHITECTS
LONDON, UK

This garden extension was originally commissioned as a study for the parents, but was quickly taken over by the kids to become 'a hotdesking environment for a family of five'. As the client wanted it to be invisible from the other side of the canal, architect Gianni Botsford approached this project as an exercise in dematerialization. Built from clear glass and camouflaged with a white fritted pattern, the frameless structure blends into the white façade.

Inside, the 8.3 m² (89.3 sq ft) space accommodates a small library and a study but maintains a sense of space due to the uniform use of seamless Corian surfaces and the transparent enclosure that opens the tiny box towards the garden and the sky. To minimize its exterior size, the extension is partly sunk into the ground, which places the desk at the same level as the garden, and the benches flush with the apartment's floor.

EXTENSION FOR A CELLIST

CUT ARCHITECTURES
CHAVILLE, FRANCE

In addition to renovating this detached single-family house in a Parisian suburb, the owner – a cellist – needed an extension that she could use as her rehearsal room. Benjamin Clarens and Yann Martin from CUT architectures responded by inserting a concrete volume between the walls of this and the adjacent house, which has produced not only a dual-aspect rehearsal room, but also a parking garage beneath. Two years later, the team returned to insert a further extension on the other side, providing a study room and a new entrance to the house. The two extensions share similar design traits, such as a full-height window enclosed in a concrete frame, and an expanded aluminium mesh frontage on the ground floor. The second extension features a large skylight and a staircase in yellow lacquered steel, with its railings used to reinforce the study desk made from the same material.

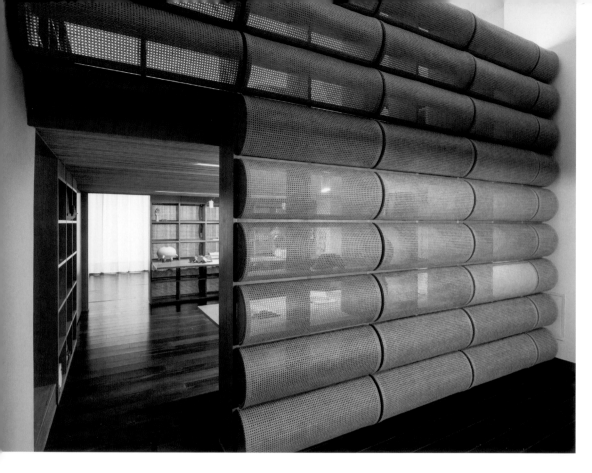

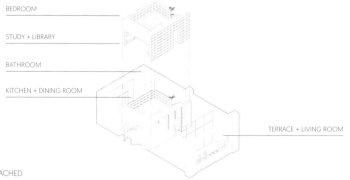

BEDROOM

STUDY + LIBRARY

BATHROOM

KITCHEN + DINING ROOM

TERRACE + LIVING ROOM

CASA CP

NORMAL
BUENOS AIRES, ARGENTINA

This family residence in a converted industrial warehouse lacked a place where one could retreat and relax. The client expected Martin Huberman and his team at Buenos Aires-based studio Normal to transform the building's loft 'into a sort of Fortress of Solitude', a reference to Superman's distant getaway. An alternative to a more conventional 'man cave'-style sanctuary, his project is structured around the library. 'We drew inspiration from the old typology of libraries, when they were entire rooms that housed the expansive intellectual universes of their owners,' Huberman says. The grid-based frame forms an enclosure at the centre of the loft; its bookcase walls contain a study topped by a bedroom deck and define areas for dining and relaxing on two opposite sides. Exterior cladding in rounded rattan wicker modules creates a softer feel, like a 'permeable cave'.

EXTENSION HOUSE VB4

DMVA
BRECHT, BELGIUM

In a former recreation area recently approved for full residential use, Belgian architecture firm dmvA has converted a vacation house into a permanent dwelling. The 54 m² (581 sq ft) cottage required an extension that would comply with the area's specific building regulations and at the same time be a convincing match to the existing A-frame structure. The resulting design uses the same kind of timber frame as the main volume, and even exposes it at the point where the old and new parts converge. On a 26 m² (280 sq ft) footprint, the extension – with its all-white interior – hosts the workspace complete with a library, the bathroom and the new entrance to the house. Glazed front and rear façades allow for natural views, while a sliding partition screen (seen at the back of the photo above) can close off the road-facing façade as necessary.

TOWNHOUSE

ELDING OSCARSON
LANDSKRONA, SWEDEN

Located on a tiny, 75 m² [807 sq ft] plot that remained empty for some 50 years, this townhouse with its rectangular frontage, pristine white façades and large square windows has been thoughtfully inserted into the context of a little Swedish town. It has the triple aim of creating a strong presence while highlighting both the project's inner clarity and the beauty of its motley, small-scale surroundings. The clients, a couple who run a café and are involved in the arts, planned to use their new house as a gallery and therefore 'needed walls for art, not for privacy'. The architects responded with a largely see-through, three-storey, open-plan design with minimal partitions and a home office located in a separate building across a small garden.

SHADOW SHED

NEIL DUSHEIKO ARCHITECTS
LONDON, UK

Neil Dusheiko created this garden pavilion for a London-based psychiatrist who needed an addition to her Victorian-era house for receiving clients during the day and practising yoga at night. The design draws on the familiar shed typology and complies with the conservation department's requirement for a material that would feel 'quiet and ubiquitous in the back garden'. The timber cladding was burned using a traditional Japanese technique that endows wood with fire- and rot-resistant properties – not to mention a richly textured, charred surface. The floor is sunk into the earth to reduce the pavilion's exterior size. The plywood interior with poured resin flooring is lit by warm, recessed LED lights; additional light comes from a constellation of pinholes in the ceiling to help transform the ambience inside this small, multipurpose shed.

THE RUG ROOM

NIC HOWETT ARCHITECT
LONDON, UK

Architect Nic Howett has crafted a standalone workspace on a seemingly unbuildable site, for a client who, on her retirement, decided to focus on designing rag rugs and so needed 'a place to think and work'. Erected close to the end of a strip-like, long and extremely narrow garden, the workshop is a double-layer, self-supporting plywood structure sheathed in a Corten steel shell. In addition to storage for books and materials, the 8 m² (86 sq ft) cabin boasts two full-height windows – one of them fitted with a wall-to-wall work surface – offering views in opposite directions. Two doors lead towards the house and to a micro-garden at the rear. With on-site construction ruled out by definition, Howett prefabricated his design in a joiner's workshop and delivered it to the client as an assembly kit, with components small enough to be manoeuvred through the house and down a narrow staircase.

ZEN HOUSES

PETR STOLÍN ARCHITEKT
LIBEREC, CZECH REPUBLIC

Czech architects Petr Stolín and Alena Mičeková were challenged to design an ultra-simple building system for residential use, based on standard structural insulated panels (an industrially manufactured material, in which an insulating foam core is sandwiched between two flakeboard sheets). The scheme consists of two identically sized, rectangular two-storey volumes, a residence and a studio, with transparent acrylic cladding mounted on a wooden frame. Set parallel to each other, the buildings have generous window openings that frame beautiful exterior views, but also enable a visual contact between the 'home' and 'work' realms. Austere interiors – white for the studio and black for the residence – maintain a sense of space despite the buildings being merely 3 m (9.8 ft) wide. The minimized contrast between the home and the office 'proves that the system can adapt to a variety of individual solutions', Stolín comments.

CORK STUDY

SURMAN WESTON
LONDON, UK

London-based Surman Weston architects designed a workspace for a musician and seamstress couple. Situated in the clients' garden – and occupying almost its entire width – the 13 m² (140 sq ft) studio has a single-material interior, with both the walls and the furniture made from birch plywood. Eco-friendly expanded cork blocks are used as external cladding that serves the triple purpose of weatherproofing, and providing thermal and acoustic insulation. The 'earthy quality of the thick cork combined with wild flower roof also helps nestle the building into its organic green surroundings', the team adds. A skylight provides generous natural lighting for the shared desk, divided in two by a central slot window. A wide, fully retractable pocket door opens the inner space towards the outdoors.

NEAR HOUSE

MOUNT FUJI ARCHITECTS
TOKYO, JAPAN

Sited between architecture and furniture, the two volumes that together constitute the so-called 'Near House' form the architects' response to a challenging L-shaped site in one of Tokyo's dense residential areas. A narrow strip of land leads to the main, set-back part of the plot – yet, to architect Masahiro Harada, this slit-like space between two neighbouring houses gave an impression of closeness, rather than of oppressive tightness. Having split the residential functions between two distinct buildings, he designed a gatehouse hosting the street entrance, library and study, and the main house containing the bedroom, bathroom, kitchen and living area. The courtyard feels like a room that connects the two houses, whose facing façades are generously glazed. The post-and-beam structure in bonded wood forms a grid, with dimensions based on a standard Japanese storage shelf size; the house seems to be made of shelves, which enhances the sense of intimacy.

THE TWO HOUSES, FIRST-FLOOR PLAN:
1 GATEHOUSE: STUDY
2 MAIN HOUSE: KITCHEN/LIVING SPACE

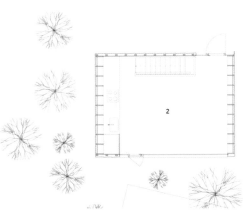

WRITER'S SHED

WESTON SURMAN & DEANE ARCHITECTURE
LONDON, UK

This backyard studio by Weston Surman & Deane architects, commissioned by an author and illustrator, was intended to provide the client with a functional workspace and to reflect his passion for children's literature and mythology. The front façade, which glows like a lantern, together with the pitched roof, shingle cladding, log store and woodburning stove all create the effect of a 'fairy-tale hut at the bottom of the garden'. The asymmetrical roof pitch allows for a large, north-facing skylight above the writing nook, while the see-through frontage made from cedar slats is backed by a second façade in frameless glass, forming a comfortable covered verandah. Inside, custom bookshelves meander around the stove and incorporate an antique sink. The materials – oiled flakeboard for the shelves and flooring, painted pine for the walls – are modest, resilient, and will age well.

WRITING PAVILION

ARCHITENSIONS
BROOKLYN, NEW YORK

In this garden studio for a creative couple, Alessandro Orsini and Nick Roseboro of Brooklyn-based firm Architensions sculpted the 6.3 m² (68 sq ft) space to create optimal lighting conditions and the atmosphere of 'immersive solitude' necessary for writing and drawing. The project was also an occasion to explore the relationship between people and nature in an urban setting. Set on a concrete plinth and raised slightly off the ground, the cabin has a glass door, and an unobtrusive exterior and light-filled interior. This is achieved via external cladding in black-stained cedar and an interior that is uniformly lined with natural pine plywood and faceted to bring in and amplify natural light. The roof is shaped to serve as a light well, open to the trees and the sky. Minimalist furnishings consist of a folding desk and a chair.

PANKHASARI
RETREAT

CARLO RATTI ASSOCIATI & MICHELE BONINO
PANKHASARI, INDIA

'For the first time in history, it might be possible to locate on a mountaintop and to maintain intimate, real-time and realistic contact with business or other associates.' So said urban designer Melvin Webber, who, back in the 1970s, envisioned new living models enabled by digital technologies. The team behind this Pankhasari retreat had his words in mind in their proposal for a co-living and co-working complex in the Indian Himalayas. As long as there is an Internet connection, such places do not need to be limited to urbanized areas, but can be located in 'the planet's most remote and beautiful corners' – as long as they remain environmentally respectful. Carlo Ratti and his design and innovation practice were joined by architect Michele Bonino and over 20 other professionals, including the engineering team tasked with ensuring a high-speed broadband connection, and practitioners and craftspeople from the area, who brought local knowledge to the project.

PROJECT CREDITS

Desk Pad [14]
Design: Eric Degenhardt
(eric-degenhardt.com)
Production: Boewer (boewer.com)

Longue [15]
Design: Massimo Mariani
(massimomariani.co.uk)
Production: Targa Italia (targaitalia.it)

22 m² Apartment [16]
Taipei, Taiwan
Design: A Little Design
(facebook.com/Design.A.Little)

Enchord Table [18]
Design: Industrial Facility
(industrialfacility.co.uk)
Production: Herman Miller
(hermanmiller.com)

AA Desk [19]
Design: Spant Studio (spant.dk)
Production: Woud (woud.dk)

Apartment in Puteaux [20]
Puteaux, France
Design: Graal Architecture
(graalarchitecture.com)

Hack Family [21]
Design: Konstantin Grcic
(konstantin-grcic.com)
Production: Vitra (vitra.com)

Interior for Students [22]
Moscow, Russia
Design: Ruetemple (ruetemple.ru)

Juliette aux Combles [24]
Montreal, Canada
Design: L. McComber (lmccomber.ca)

Loft MM [26]
Bilzen, Belgium
Design: C.T. Architects (ctarchitects.be)

Writer's Block [28]
Los Angeles, California
Design: CHA:COL (chacol.net)

Doehler [30]
Brooklyn, New York
Design: SABO Project (sabo-project.com)

A Room for Two [32]
London, UK
Design: Studio Ben Allen
(studiobenallen.com)

Kevin [34]
Hong Kong, China
Design: JAAK Design (jaak.co)

Apartment XIV [36]
Paris, France
Design: Studio Razavi Architecture
(studiorazavi.com)

Toy Loft [38]
Los Angeles, California
Design: CHA:COL (chacol.net)

Luoto [40]
Design: Sami Rintala (ri-eg.com)
Production: Danese Milano
(danesemilano.com)

The Rental [42]
Sydney, Australia
Design: Nicholas Gurney
(nicholasgurney.com.au)

Dengshikou Hutong [44]
Beijing, China
Design: B.L.U.E. Architecture Studio
(b-l-u-e.net)

Flat 8 [46]
Hong Kong, China
Design: DEFT (designeightfivetwo.com)

Red Nest [48]
Paris, France
Design: Coudamy Architectures
(coudamyarchitectures.com)

Islington Micro Flat [50]
London, UK
Design: CIAO (ciao.archi)

Five To One Apartment [52]
New York, New York
Design: Michael K. Chen Architecture
(mkca.com)

All I Own House [54]
Madrid, Spain
Design: formerly PKMN Architectures,
now ENORME Studio (enormestudio.es)
& EEESTUDIO (eeestudio.es)

Home/Studio Kilburn Lane [110]
London, UK
Design: Studio McLeod
[studiomcleod.com]

Area [116]
Design: Alain Gilles [alaingilles.com]
Production: Magnitude [magnitude.be]

Deskbox [117]
Design: Raw Edges [raw-edges.com]
Production: Arco [arco.nl]

FLKS [118]
Design: Kapteinbolt [kapteinbolt.nl]

Wall [119]
Design: Gilles Belley [gillesbelley.fr]

Flatbox [120], Flatmate [121]
Design: Michael Hilgers [michaelhilgers.de]
Production: Müller Möbelwerkstätten
[muellermoebel.de]

Duotable [122]
Design: Michael Hilgers [michaelhilgers.de]
Production: Urban Favourites
[urbanfavourites.de]

Setup [123]
Design: Michael Hilgers [michaelhilgers.de]
Production: Müller Möbelwerkstätten
[muellermoebel.de]

Home-Studio MQ 60 [124]
Pescara, Italy
Design: MKS architetti [mksarchitetti.it]

Plaza Kennedy Apartment [126]
Barcelona, Spain
Design: Anna & Eugeni Bach
[annaeugenibach.com]

Workroom [128]
Moscow, Russia
Design: Ruetemple [ruetemple.ru]

Ben Gurion Boulevard Apartment [130]
Tel Aviv, Israel
Design: Dori-Design [dori-design.com]

SS Penthouse [132]
Antwerp, Belgium
Design: De Meester Vliegen
[demeestervliegen.com]

Les Enfants Rouges [134]
Paris, France
Design: Ubalt Architectes
[ubalt-architectes.com]

Screen House [136]
London, UK
Design: Studio Ben Allen
[studiobenallen.com]

Domestic Fences [138]
Milan, Italy
Design: FuGa_Officina dell'Architettura
[fugaunderscore.net]

Illustrator's Apartment [140]
São Paulo, Brazil
Design: Claudia Bresciani & Júlia Risi
[juliarisi.com]

Biombombastic [142]
Madrid, Spain
Design: ELII [elii.es]

Domino Loft [144]
San Francisco, California
Design: Peter Suen [fiftharch.com]
& Charles Irby [icosadesign.com]

Home & Office [146]
Florence, Italy
Design: Roberto Monsani &
Silvia Allori [silviaallori.it]

Inhabited Wooden Walls [148]
Geneva, Switzerland
Design: Aurélie Monet Kasisi
[monetkasisi.ch]

Susaloon [150]
Madrid, Spain
Design: ELII [elii.es]

Harry [152]
Paris, France
Design: Dixneufcentquatrevingtsix [19-86.fr]

Compact Living [154]
Copenhagen, Denmark
Design: Spacon & X [spaconandx.com]

Unfolding Apartment [156]
New York, New York
Design: Michael K. Chen Architecture
[mkca.com]

Attic Transformer [158]
New York, New York
Design: Michael K. Chen Architecture
[mkca.com]

Artist Studio [160]
Tel Aviv, Israel
Design: RUST architects [rustarch.com],
formerly Studio Raanan Stern

Urban Hermitage [162]
London, UK
Design: Spheron Architects
[spheronarchitects.co.uk]

F-Residence [226]
Gifu, Japan
Design: Shinichi Ogawa & Associates
[shinichiogawa.com]

SS Garden Pavilion [228]
Antwerp, Belgium
Design: De Meester Vliegen
[demeestervliegen.com]

Diapositive [230]
Design: Ronan & Erwan Bouroullec
[bouroullec.com]
Production: Glas Italia [glasitalia.com]

Koloro Desk [231]
Design: Torafu Architects [torafu.com]
Production: Ichiro [ichirodesign.jp]

Area, Block [232]
Design: Gilles Belley [gillesbelley.fr]

Living Cube [234]
Design: Till Könneker [tillkoenneker.work]
& Dana Loftus
Production: Living Cube
[livingcube.furniture]

Work and Live [236]
Tel Aviv, Israel
Design: RUST architects [rustarch.com]

Artillery Mansions [238]
London, UK
Design: FORMstudio [formstudio.co.uk]

White on White [240]
London, UK
Design: Gianni Botsford Architects
[giannibotsford.com]

Extension for a Cellist [242]
Chaville, France
Design: CUT architectures
[cut-architectures.com]

Casa CP [244]
Buenos Aires, Argentina
Design: Normal™ [normal.com.ar]

Extension House vB4 [246]
Brecht, Belgium
Design: dmvA architecten
[dmva-architecten.be]

Townhouse [248]
Landskrona, Sweden
Design: Elding Oscarson
[eldingoscarson.com]

Shadow Shed [250]
London, UK
Design: Neil Dusheiko Architects
[neildusheiko.com]

The Rug Room [252]
London, UK
Design: Nic Howett Architect
[nichowett.co.uk]

Zen Houses [254]
Liberec, Czech Republic
Design: Petr Stolín Architekt [stolin58.com]

Cork Study [256]
London, UK
Design: Surman Weston
[surmanweston.com]

Near House [258]
Tokyo, Japan
Design: Mount Fuji Architects
[fuji-studio.jp]

Writer's Shed [260]
London, UK
Design: formerly Weston Surman &
Deane Architecture, now Surman Weston
[surmanweston.com]

Writing Pavilion [262]
Brooklyn, New York
Design: Architensions [architensions.com]

Pankhasari Retreat [264]
Pankhasari valley, West Bengal, India
Design: Carlo Ratti Associati [carloratti.com]
with Michele Bonino
Local architect: Ashish Sharan Lal / Alleya &
Associates [alleyacom.wordpress.com]

DESIGNERS

On the cover: Koloro desk, by Torafu Architects; *Back, clockwise from top left* Puzzle Wall, by Spacon & X; Room on the Roof, by i29 Interior Architects; All I Own Home, by PKMN Architectures; Doehler, by SABO Project

HomeWork: Design Solutions for Working from Home © 2018 Anna Yudina

Designed by Anna Yudina

First published in 2018 in the United States of America by Thames & Hudson Inc., 500 Fifth Avenue, New York, New York 10110

www.thamesandhudsonusa.com

Library of Congress Control Number 2017945550

ISBN 978-0-500-51980-6

Printed and bound in China by C&C Offset Printing Co. Ltd